*Just the Other Day*

by *WARD MOREHOUSE*

### *books*

FORTY-FIVE MINUTES PAST EIGHT
AMERICAN REVEILLE
GEORGE M. COHAN—*Prince of the American Theater*
MATINEE TOMORROW
JUST THE OTHER DAY—*From Yellow Pines to Broadway*

### *plays*

GENTLEMEN OF THE PRESS
MISS QUIS
NEW YORK TOWN

# Just
# the Other
# Day

~~~~~~~~~

*from Yellow Pines to Broadway*

*by* **WARD MOREHOUSE**

*McGraw-Hill Book Company, Inc.*

NEW YORK   TORONTO   LONDON

## JUST THE OTHER DAY

Library of Congress Catalog Card Number: 53–5190

Published by the McGraw-Hill Book Company, Inc.

Printed in the United States of America

*To Becky*
*for coming into my life*
*and to*
*Martha Morehouse Bowen*
*who did so very much*
*to brighten my boyhood years*

## chapter one

~~~~~~~~~~~~~

THE WINTERS dragged on, and somehow
passed; the summers went quickly. They were cherished. In
the summertime the melancholy willows caressed the tiny and
gurgling eddies in the south Georgia rivers, some of which
were blue-black and swift; others were sluggish and copper-
colored, sometimes as motionless as millponds. Blue hydrangeas were radiantly in bloom beside front-veranda steps and in
the corners of front lawns. There was a hammock at one end
of a vine-shaded veranda and a swing at the other, and from
the parlor phonograph, a Victor with the big horn, there came
the brazen lilt of "Waltz Me Around Again, Willie" or the
soulful strains of "I Wonder Who's Kissing Her Now."

Little towns in the yellow-pine and turpentine country
sizzled in the heat of July and August. In the mornings, as the
workday began, the men of business were moderately brisk.
The proprietor of the City Café matched Doc, who ran the
drugstore, for Coca-Colas as they stood together at the soda
fountain; the editor of the local weekly cackled pleasantly in

exchanging comment with the postmaster, and the hardware dealer predicted, more or less cheerfully, that everybody was in for another scorcher. At 9 A.M. nobody minded particularly. People were busy; life would go on.

But by midday, as the tracks of the Atlantic Coast Line glinted in the stifling heat, the tempo slowed, a small boy circled aimlessly on his new bicycle, and an aging Negro, gnarled and shrunken, who did odd jobs about the railroad station, sought the shade and comparative coolness of the waiting room marked "White" for his siesta. A vast inertia, a communicable drowsiness, descended upon the entire region. There was now scarcely a stir in the palmettos, barely a quiver in the long-leaf pines. Resistance to the 98-degree heat vanished. Streets became deserted and porches unoccupied; stores were empty—some were closed—and for about two hours all business was suspended, with Courthouse Square in something of a stupor.

And then, suddenly, life began again. Shopkeepers emerged from their houses and returned to work, refreshed by the noontime nap. Traffic reappeared in the streets—buggies, two-wheeled carts, surreys, traps, farm wagons, and automobiles here and there, one of the newer models belonging to the energetic and voluble drummer who had come down all the way from Atlanta. By nightfall, the temperature had fallen a few degrees, a slight breeze had come up, rain threatened, and the fierce discomforts of a few hours before were entirely forgotten.

Many of the towns that I knew in Georgia were built around the big, red-brick, white-columned courthouses; the square was

2

fringed by business establishments—the bank, the drugstore, the clothing store, the print shop, the café, the barbershop, the post office, the hardware store. The livery stable was around the corner and down the street. As the years passed, and as the automobile age asserted itself, the gas station came along, the movie theater appeared, and space was found for the beauty shoppe. There were few cars in Guyton and an automobile seldom appeared in Olympia, the places I knew best. When Rock, the proud chestnut-sorrel and an oversensitive Kentucky thoroughbred, which belonged to my Olympia aunt, first set eyes upon a mechanical monstrosity he bolted into the pine woods, dragging the surrey right after him. On previous runaways he had been startled by the clamorous arrival of the dinky Georgia & Florida train, on its way from Valdosta to Madison, Florida, or by a blast from the asthmatic locomotive of a logging train, hauling fresh-cut timber to Olympia's big sawmill.

Those were years of stereopticon slides, sugar-cane grindings, scuppernong picking; of Gibson-girl drawings, George Barr McCutcheon's *Nedra* and *Beverly of Graustark*; summers of buggy rides, Sunday-school picnics, and swimming in pine-woods ponds and in railroad culverts. There were water lilies and lily pads in the glassy millponds; livestock—horses, cattle, pigs, goats—ran loose, roaming unconcernedly alongside the railroad tracks. Grownups rocked sedately on those shady front porches and talked, with sighs, smiles, chuckles, and pauses, of the inconsequentials of an untroubled world—in the aftermath of the Russo-Japanese War, William Jennings Bryan, Sarah Bernhardt, and tandem bicycles and the conquest of

3

the North Pole; of T. R. and suffragettes and *St. Elmo* and *The Port of Missing Men*. They gathered about the piano in a corner of the sacred front parlor and sang "Sweet Genevieve" and "In the Good Old Summertime"; they talked around the dinner table of the small excitements in their immediate world and gorged themselves upon fried chicken and rice with egg gravy, country ham and country butter, beaten biscuits and corn on the cob, watermelon and strawberry shortcake made with berries from the patch in the garden just beyond the chicken yard.

I knew the rivers of that south Georgia country—the Savannah, swollen and muddy and yellow; the Ogeechee, very shallow in spots, deep in others, with golden, sandy banks, forever eddying and willow-lined; the coiling Withlacoochee, flowing along swiftly at the Georgia–Florida line, and that stream of unsurpassed beauty known as the Altamaha. I went to numerous towns during those hot and wonderful summers. . . . Flovilla, up in Georgia's red-clay regions, on the way to Atlanta; Thomasville, snug at the bottom of the state, to which wealthy sportsmen from the North went for bobwhite quail, and in which Uncle Jim Dillon had a musty grain and feed store and my serene Aunt Jennie gave her care to her roses and her beautiful hydrangeas. There was Boston, just to the north of the Florida line, where the fresh milk at Aunt Gussie's table was brought direct from the cow in its back-yard stall, and there was the upstate Indian Springs, to which people came from all of Georgia's counties to drink its supposedly healthy sulfur water. It was during a day of picnicking at Indian Springs that I was stung by a wasp, fell out of a chair, suffered

4

a deep gash in my chin, and bled for an hour. A doctor was summoned, stitches were required, and everybody became so upset by the incident the family returned to south Georgia the very next day, notwithstanding the fact that board had been paid in nearby Flovilla for an entire week.

Indian Springs, Flovilla, Thomasville and Boston, Jesup and Valdosta—those were names of magic in my boyhood, but Guyton and Olympia were the towns I visited most frequently. Guyton, in Effingham County, bearing the name of one Archibald Guyton, postmaster in its early days, and 30 miles from my home city of Savannah, was always a place for a stay of some weeks during summertime holidays, and so was Olympia, south of Valdosta, down in Lowndes County and only half a mile or so from the enchanting Withlacoochee. Olympia came to hold first place in my affections. For one reason, of course, because visiting Olympia, lying 170-odd miles to the southwest of Savannah, became a journey of spectacular proportions. For another, it was at Olympia that my favorite relative, the aunt we called Sister Mattie, lived and had the finest house in town.

Guyton was small, dusty, and hot, unshielded against the south Georgia sun. It was incorporated in 1886; it's on the Central of Georgia's Savannah-to-Atlanta run, and the old wood burners used to screech through. During my childhood visits there were legends of many of the town's characters, one of whom was a Dr. Long, who had a drugstore and won the affection of Guytonians because he would stand behind the soda counter and fan the flies away as his customers sipped their milk shakes.

5

I made my trips to Guyton by horse and buggy—a long and hard 30 miles it was—once or twice by bicycle, and once on foot, which seemed to require a good part of a lifetime. But most of the Savannah-to-Guyton journeys were accomplished via the sooty, jerky, impulsive accommodation train that was known as the *Shoo-Fly*, and on which Cousin Herschel Powers, a kindly man with a drooping white mustache, was the conductor. The *Shoo-Fly* was as hospitable a carrier as the American railways have ever known. It slowed down, with no show of petulance, to clear the tracks of unheeding cattle; it made ungrudging stops at the stations along the route— Pooler, Meldrim, Marlow, Eden, Pineora—and once it did stop it was never in a hurry to get going again.

Cousin Agnes ran a boardinghouse in Guyton. She had bony arms and very long fingers; she was swarthy and tight-skinned, and her gray-black hair was always parted severely in the middle and pulled down flat to her ears. Her husband, Andrew Simmons, was a farmer and was always bringing loads of watermelons to the house. These were cut by Cousin Agnes with an expert hand. She was also a specialist in country butter, and there was a clamor for her baked koghloaf, raisin-filled and cakelike. Cousin Agnes was not a bitter woman but she was frequently grim, and she had reason to be. Her grown daughter, Maud, had been taken with scarlet fever at the age of five, and throughout her short and terrible life— she was dead before she was thirty—her mind was that of a child. Cousin Agnes's two sons were Dan and Jim. Dan was a lively boy, likable, dark, and good-looking, and it was obvious to everyone that he was his mother's first love. A hardy

6

and strong-willed woman, Cousin Agnes, and I recall my surprise when I saw her eyes filled with tears. She had just received the news of Dan's tragic end: he had been burned to death in his hotel room in a south Georgia fire. Some years later, after Cousin Agnes had passed on, her son Jim was lying in his coffin, dead of natural causes, when the house caught fire. Only the quick action of a swarm of children from a nearby school checked the blaze before it reached Jim in the somber front parlor.

In Guyton there were always watermelon cuttings, the farm-wagon trips to the Ogeechee River for fishing, sugar-cane grindings—achieved by the hitching of a mule to a pole that was attached to the cane mill and driving him round and round, as on a merry-go-round, as someone stood by and fed the sugar-cane stalks into a trough which carried the cane juice into an enormous sirup-making vat—and always those expeditions to the Big Culvert. The Wells boys, J. T. and Duncan, generally the first to make the high dive from the railroad ties into the swimming hole beside the Central of Georgia tracks, stay in my memory. So do Cousin Eula Powers, dark-haired and good-looking, who wore peekaboo shirtwaists and had a soft voice and a definite elegance; Miss Birdie Neidlinger, a crack rifle shot who always seemed to be reading, and never finishing, *Quo Vadis, David Harum,* and *When Knighthood Was in Flower.* A summertime month in Guyton always included coon hunting, possum hunting, and frolicking with the pack of fine, floppy-eared foxhounds that belonged to the Neidlingers. I've had great respect for some dogs that I've owned in my time, certainly for a Norwegian elkhound and for an acrobatic wire-haired named Dixie, but the most magnificent dog I've ever known was the foxhound Ring, leader of the Neidlinger pack, an animal that had the respect and awe of the entire town of Guyton and one of such strength and daring he once made a remarkable leap from the ground to the top of a scuppernong arbor. I saw him do it.

Notwithstanding all the activity that the hot and unkempt little town of Guyton offered every summer, it never provided the sheer excitement that Olympia did. Olympia, with its great sawmill and its Blue Sink swimming hole, mysterious, circular, and seemingly bottomless, was the scene of more drama. And Sister Mattie, with her pompadour and her Gibson-girl profile, her endless store of folklore, her knowledge of the community, her sustained and diverting chatter, was a great attraction in herself. She fascinated me.

I could never wait for those annual trips to Lowndes County to begin. There always seemed to be endless weeks of unnecessary preparation. Letters were exchanged between Savannah and Olympia; letters from my mother to the Bowens, letters to my mother from that indulgent Olympia aunt, wife of the impressive S. W. Bowen, vice-president and general manager of the West Yellow Pine Company, manufacturers of rough and dressed yellow-pine lumber. Letters in which Savannah asked Olympia, over and over again, if Olympia was sure my coming would cause no inconvenience; hospitable replies that urged immediate departure. Then, at last, the exact date would be decided upon. My mother would sigh, "Well, Mattie seems to mean it." My clothes would be packed, a half-an-hour task that was not completed in less than three days; a train-trip lunch was prepared, and then there'd be the usual admonitions: "don't put your head out of the window," "don't go out on the platform," "don't leave the station at Valdosta until they're there to meet you," "don't—don't—don't." Then, finally, I'd be hustled off to Savannah's Union Station and kissed good-by ten or twenty times. I'd always welcome that long-drawn-out and melancholy call, "all ab-o-o-a-a-rd," which was done with all the histrionics at the conductor's command. The ACL was then off on the thrilling run to Valdosta, a marketing center for south Georgia and north Florida farmers.

The *Coast Line* rattled along over sun-scorched tracks, hurtling past swamps and pools of black, stagnant water, past sawmills and great conical piles of sawdust and mile after mile of yellow-pine forest, on through the turpentine country, making stops along the route. There were the names of the towns spelled out in bold and dramatic station legends—Jesup, Ludowici, Blackshear, Waycross. There was always Jesup, vexatious and inevitable, and just a little hotter than any other place. People changed trains at Jesup; the pauses there seemed unnecessarily prolonged, and the town became a fixation in the minds of all south Georgia travelers. The mere mention of it at a social gathering was certain to produce mirth; Jesup-jokes were in the repertoire of stage comedians and itinerant lecturers. The *Coast Line*, once past Jesup, always seemed to move a little faster. The conductor, once the Jesup ordeal was over, was always a bit more human. He even permitted himself a smile or two as he sauntered regally through the cars.

In midafternoon, after the passing of some five hours, and

with the bustling division point of Waycross behind us, the *Coast Line* slowed down perceptibly; houses became more numerous alongside the tracks, and there was a great deal of movement in the gritty, grimy cars and in the cinder-filled, red-plush seats. A frantic tying of strings about lunch boxes— "No use to let all that good chicken go to waste," my older sister would be saying—a last-minute opening and closing of bags, a reaching into the overhead rack for such odds and ends as on-arrival presents for Sister Mattie and Uncle Solon, and then, as if on cue, the portly conductor, his run completed, his mission accomplished, and triumph in his eyes, would appear in the platform doorway and indulge himself in a pleasant and triumphant roar, "Val-l-d-dos-ta!"

There, right there beside the tracks, Sister Mattie would be standing—Sister Mattie with her eyes bright, her shirtwaist freshly ironed, her pompadour just so. Shrieks, hugs, kisses, and laughter, and then, with bags and bundles, we'd march, chattering at every step, to the nearby station of the Georgia & Florida Railroad to board the two-car-and-a-locomotive train that would bear us through 15 miles of pines, via the village of Clyattville, to the magic of the sawmill settlement that was known as Olympia.

My Aunt Mattie, born Martha Morehouse in Guyton and daughter of that resolute and devil-pursuing Methodist preacher, the Reverend Norman David Morehouse, had come down to south Georgia to reign as first lady of Olympia after her marriage to Solon W. Bowen, of Freedonia, Alabama, the son of a merchant. Uncle Solon, at the time of his introduction to my aunt, was treasurer of the Wesley Monumental

Church of Savannah and was regarded as an exceptionally fine young man. He had a good job with a wholesale hardware company, but later, when he was offered a better one by the West Yellow Pine Company, he asked his bride how she'd like living in the country, the real country. "Solon," she said, "my place is to be where you are." "It might not be too easy for you," he said. "Perhaps it will be better if we had our home in Valdosta." And then she asked if that would mean that he would commute 30 miles daily by horse and buggy! He nodded. He said, "Valdosta will be more comfortable for you. Olympia is the real backwoods." She looked at him for a moment and made the decision: "All right, Solon. It will have to be the backwoods. If you're going to work in Olympia we'll live in Olympia, and I'll love it."

And she did, from the very beginning. Sister Mattie had a nervous energy that was inexhaustible and often fairly exhausting. The household duties that she assigned to herself were seemingly endless but she still found the time to read most of the sentimental novels of the day; she knew the words of all the popular songs; she never neglected her scripture reading, and always seemed fresh and eager and ready for her duties as church organist on Sundays. She was also an excellent pianist.

The Bowens, during my Olympia summers, had about a hundred and fifty chickens, two fine cows, several goats, a flock of pigeons, a vegetable garden, and a berry patch. My aunt took great pride in her strawberry shortcake and her country butter. A fresh mound of newly made country butter always seemed to be available. A churn was used for the butter-making—an earthen crock affair, with a dasher in the center. Sour milk and lots of heavy cream were poured in, the dasher pushed up and down and, after much labor, the butter "gathered," as the Negroes expressed it, and the contents of the churn were taken out and salted. That was country butter. When it was applied to thin, hot biscuits and these were served with golden-brown fried chicken, you had a meal! There were always such meals in the house of Bowen.

Uncle Solon, quite the big man of the community and actually very friendly and affable, was given to long and somewhat frightening periods of silence at mealtime—Sister Mattie often remarked that he never began thinking of his mill until he sat down to eat—and as he remained mute she went along with her role of hostess and chatterbox. Solon Bowen had a black mustache and he kept it neat. He wore good clothes, was never without a white piqué waistcoat on Sundays—he was superintendent of the Sunday school—always said grace before meals, and often would not utter another word until the dessert was passed.

Uncle Solon took to the lumber business in Lowndes County with great relish. He had a downright affection for the company's locomotives—numbers 101, 120, and 121—and for the engineers, Riley Shaw and Emery Welch. Those redoubtable locomotives hauled in the timber after it had been toppled by crosscut saws and loaded onto the flatcars. The logs were taken to the edge of the big millpond and dumped in and floated until they were drawn up into the mill by heavy chains and processed. Olympia's finished lumber was sent to all parts of the country, and whenever a bustling stranger stepped off the train from Valdosta and asked for the whereabouts of Mrs. Lee's boardinghouse, it was generally conceded that another lumber buyer had found his way to our little town.

Sister Mattie and Uncle Solon, as I saw them and knew them for a month in every year and over a period of six or seven years, were enormously interesting people in a peculiarly fascinating locale. In the blurring memories of passing years they have appeared as the principal characters in a summertime dream sequence, but during those summers of 1907–1913, they had reality and vitality. Uncle Solon seemed to me to be a man of vast wisdom and decisiveness; I often interpreted his brevity of speech for a definite austerity. But I liked him. And I gave my heart to my aunt without reservation. I found her loquacity enjoyable and her knowledge of all things, from Georgia folklore to names of all the battles won by the Confederacy, as well as those that it came near winning, entertaining and stimulating. I don't suppose I ever came to regard the Bowens as relatives. They were more than that. They were people identified with a very happy period in my life, and with a pine-woods town that I had come to love.

There were others of the Lowndes County scene who made great impressions upon me. Rosabelle Hatton, gaunt and laconic, who wore eyeglasses and dressed like a man, could walk 10 miles without tiring. She knew how to ride and how to fish; she liked hunting and had been known to bring down two quail, flitting through the pines, after the rise of a covey. There was the friendly Negro, Uncle Peter, who must have been ninety. He was an employee of the West Yellow Pine

Company, which operated a sawmill, a shingle mill, a planing mill, and dry kiln and confined itself exclusively to golden yellow pine. He went to the plant early one morning to sharpen his ax and got caught in the great belt that ran the machinery and was torn to bits. And there was, of course, Mr. Barnard, who presided gingerly at the general store, known as the Commissary, which got the trade of all of the company's three hundred employees. I often went to the Commissary for Sister Mattie, but on the day that she gave me a particularly long list I appeared before Mr. Barnard without it. "Look in all your pockets," he said. I did, and with no success. "All right, son," he said. "When you were in here last week I gave you sugar, flour, lard, side meat, soap, rice, grits, ketchup, and Coca-Colas, and I threw in a few fishhooks. I'll repeat that order. I'll give you some advice, too. On your way back home don't stop by to see that girl Beulah. If you do, Mrs. Bowen will never get her groceries."

The beauty of Olympia's pine woods had the name of Alice. She was shapely, full-breasted, and coquettish, and her purpose in life was that of bewitching every male in the county, teen-agers and graybeards included. I was by no means indifferent to Miss Alice's beguiling ways, but I somehow found myself hopelessly, desperately in love, at the age of twelve, with a summertime visitor in Alice's home—blond, blue-eyed Beulah from Waycross. Beulah was good-looking, spoiled, irresistible, and cold, "cold" being the considered judgment of the youth of Olympia after she had shown herself uncooperative and reluctant when called upon to yield to the victors in parlor kissing games.

I got my first and quite unsettling glimpse of Beulah through the screen of the Bowen front door when she stood on the porch after ringing the bell. It was a hot July morning; the Bowens had gone to Valdosta, and I was alone in the house. I was far back in the hall when I heard the bell but stopped in my tracks as I saw the vision on porch—curls, curves, blue eyes, serene face, bright new dress. I just stood there for a half minute and then went eagerly, a little too eagerly, to the door, flung open the screen, and said, a little roughly, "Good morning." She hesitated, fell back a step, and stammered, "Is Mrs. Bowen in?" No, I said, everybody was out; everybody had gone to the city. I was Ward, Mrs. Bowen's nephew. Yes, she said— and another half-step backward—she knew. Wouldn't she come in? No, she was in a great hurry; she had just come to ask the Bowens—and I was also invited—to a party at her house the next afternoon. Then I blurted out, "Yes! Yes! We'll certainly be there." She murmured a thank-you, turned quickly, and went down the walk and out the gate. I called to her, "Won't you come in and stay for a while?" She stopped sharply, turned, and said gravely, "Not now, thank you. Next time." And she was gone. She never came alone again to the Bowen house.

Beulah's aloofness always seemed to be in evidence except when she was in the presence of my young cousin, Walker, the Bowens's only child, Joe Roberts, the red-headed and vital young man who worked at the mill office, and Dr. Quillian, the general practitioner. Joe Roberts, who regarded Uncle Solon as a greater man than President Taft, was a privileged caller at the Bowen home. Most of those who came to see the

Bowens—and it was a procession so unending that there was afternoon "company" nearly every day in the week—were received on the broad veranda and served cake and iced tea, but Joe Roberts was always permitted within the confines of the "parlor" when he called upon Sister Mattie to pay his respects and tell her of this and that of the problems of the mill-workers. "I simply love for Joe to come in and chat," my aunt would say, but it seemed to me that most of Joe's time on those little visits was spent in nodding understandingly as Sister Mattie jabbered on—always listening perfectly, never once fingering the fringe on the red plush sofa, never taking his eyes from Sister Mattie's face. Perhaps he never really knew that great ancestral portraits, oval and oblong, hung somberly from the parlor's walls; that stereopticon slides and the "games"— lotto and dominoes—were to be found on the little round table over in the corner, and that the room's most treasured possession, save for the photograph of the benign Grandfather Morehouse, was a spherical glass case containing artificial flowers, which was dusted regularly and with extraordinary care. There were undoubtedly occasions of emergency when Dr. Quillian was admitted to the Bowen parlor, times when he became engaged in long and low-voiced conversation. Dr. Quillian had the quality for inspiring confidence, necessary to men of his calling, and he was also ubiquitous, as he certainly had to be. Without ubiquity, no country doctor of that time could have stayed in business and kept his peace with God. There were still tales, when I first arrived in Olympia around 1907, of the consternation that had been brought a year or so earlier when Dr. Quillian, having gone to Valdosta to fetch another doctor for a consultation, returned to Olympia in an automobile. It was the first many of the inhabitants had ever seen.

On Sunday mornings Olympia went to church; on midweek afternoons baptisms were held at the Blue Sink. Olympia's place of worship was a frame structure, standing beside the railroad tracks, out at the edge of town and toward the river. Its white paint was peeling, its windowpanes cracked, its steps were sagging, and its cupola fairly lopsided. There were frequent murmurs of building a new church, but nothing was ever done about it. Sister Mattie and Uncle Solon were resolute churchgoers. She pumped the organ with practiced and tireless feet and never seemed affected by the heat; Uncle Solon, trying to forget the affairs of the mill on the Sabbath, took over the role of the community's spiritual guardian. The women came along to services in crepes and organdies and starched ginghams and chattered on excitedly about church suppers and showers for brides-to-be and trips to Valdosta and Madison; the men, their high collars wilting and their handkerchiefs in use, talked of mill matters, of the pecan and melon crops, and sometimes touched on national events. Those Sunday sermons in Olympia always seemed needlessly and excruciatingly long to me, but I enjoyed the social spectacle, the Sabbath small talk, that always followed the benediction. . . . "Fine sermon, wasn't it?" . . . "Really, a wonderful sermon— simply wonderful." . . . "Aren't we lucky to have such a fine preacher?" . . . "Hope we can keep him; that's what I say." . . . The Bowens always lingered to exchange greetings with members of the congregation and always invited the pastor over for the big Sabbath meal. If the preacher of the day happened to be the Reverend K., a Lowndes County favorite, he never accepted without a certain remonstrance, but he always came, driving over in his own surrey, and unhitching his horse and letting it roam about the Bowen lot. The Reverend, after the intoning of an elaborate grace, achieved a full recovery from the effects of his emotional labors of the morning as he applied himself to the prodigious meal. He was generally unresisting as Sister Mattie insisted upon his having a third helping of fried chicken, and he was always a well-fed man of God when he rose to attend his horse and prepare for the 10-mile journey that was ahead of him.

Olympia's Negro baptisms were unforgettable. They were held in the blue-black and unfathomable Blue Sink, which was shallow around the edges. Those baptisms were spectacles that had their value as contributions to the community's spiritual life and certainly to its entertainment. The whites would attend in considerable number, and Uncle Solon, seldom absent, was always the spectator who would remove his hat. The Negro preacher, the Reverend Louis White, grave, dignified, unhurried, did the dipping, and every time a parishioner was ducked and came up, the wail of a chorus of Negro voices, "Jesus was a Baptist!" would echo through the pines. Sister Mattie, always doing what seemed to be just the right thing, would remain in the Bowen buggy, watching the proceedings from a distance of 50 feet, and on the way home she could tell you, and did, the name and characteristics of every church member who had been submerged.

Olympia, in that period between the end of the Russo-Japanese War and the outbreak of World War I, was a settlement of some five hundred souls, a pine-woods village that owed its existence to the presence of a prosperous sawmill; when the mill finally went out of business, Olympia vanished. The Olympia that I knew and that held me in its spell, with the coming of every July, was a place without porcelain bathtubs, without plumbing, without nickelodeons, without automobiles, but never without a certain commotion. The church suppers to which I, as a member of the Bowen household, went regularly, seemed to me to be fun. There were the train trips into Valdosta and look-in visits at the fabulous Valdez Hotel; there were expeditions to Florida and to the farming town called Madison, with its buggies and farm vehicles parked all around the courthouse square. There were hay rides, fishing trips, and river picnics. It was during a picnic beside the beautiful Withlacoochee, which took its name from an Indian, that tragedy came upon us all.

Sister Mattie was the hostess at the river party of that day, with her carefully prepared basket lunch spread out on tablecloths on the river's sandy bank, a feast characteristic of the Bowen table, and with a prodigal supply of fried chicken because everybody liked it more than anything else. The dazzling Miss Alice was there, of course, in a bathing suit, daring for the period. My demure Beulah, of the satin skin and practiced silences, sat off to one side; my older sister, Miriam, wearing a very special organdy of ribbon stripes on snowy white that had been saved for the occasion, chattered on aimlessly, with her gaze always upon Joe Roberts, notwithstanding the fact that an architect-beau who had come all the way from Savannah was hovering gloomily nearby. Joe, who was adored by practically everybody, and whose presence was necessary to guarantee the success of such an outing, had been given the day off by the company, which had acted upon my aunt's tactful suggestions. Joe, good-looking and capable and an excellent office worker, had become a vital part of Olympia's community life within the two years that he had been there. Unmarried and twenty-three, a good dancer, a violinist, and an athlete, he was the "catch" of Lowndes County. He sang an excellent baritone and was particularly effective when the hymn book called for "Holy, Holy, Holy." He went everywhere—to the baptisms, to camp meetings, to barbecues. He had a class at Sunday school and was always present at the preaching. He pitched on the mill's baseball team—his home run had defeated a brawny team from Valdosta that came down one day to play the Olympia nine—and he was known to be a fine swimmer.

It was no surprise, therefore, when he suddenly appeared in his bathing suit during Sister Mattie's river party. He received something of a cheer from the group in a circle about the tablecloth feast. He bowed to my sister Miriam and then, a little more elaborately, to the ravenous Miss Alice. He seized the shrieking and baby-faced Cousin Walker and made the motion of throwing him into the water. And then he waded in, the only bather of the day, and began swimming with sure and swift strokes for the Withlacoochee's other bank. By this time the sun had disappeared, the sky was turning black, and the river's current became suddenly swifter. There were squeals from the ladies as raindrops began to fall, squeals and a hasty mass movement toward the willows. Sister Mattie, never one to become panicky, began gathering up the party effects as the downpour increased. She paused as she was getting soaked and called to Joe Roberts, then standing on the opposite shore, to come on back. "That river," she said, "gets dangerous when it rains. . . . Alice, tell Joe to come on back. . . . Miriam, tell Joe—quick." But Miss Alice, the charmer, was then concerned about her beautiful bathing suit, never intended for the touch of water, and my sister Miriam, with a little cry, was scampering for any protection that might be provided for her crisp organdy and her bright new bonnet. Sister Mattie stood her ground. She had forgotten her tablecloths and her china and silverware; she was there in the heavy rain, watching Joe Roberts in his return crossing.

Suddenly, her hands went to her face and she moaned, "Joe! Joe! Oh, God!" Joe Roberts, the best athlete in the county, was choking, sputtering, and struggling in midstream. He disappeared. Then he came up, went down for a second time, and didn't come up again. There were shrieks from the willows. Sister Mattie, oblivious to the downpour, which had now become a cloudburst, stood transfixed at the river's edge. Then slowly, she came toward all of us and said quietly, "Somebody—somebody, go for help. Somebody, please—run. We've got to get Joe." There were tears in her eyes and she turned to the water, staring at it numbly. The black and coiling Withlacoochee had claimed a life.

There was hysteria in the willows. The rain splattered down upon our picnic baskets.

~~~~~~~~~~~~~~

## chapter two

SAVANNAH, a place of sun and sand and lacy live oaks, of charm and gentility and modernity and decadence, of booming industrialization and centuries-old stucco—Savannah, languorous and placid, with its parks and squares and monuments and wrought-iron balconies, is to be found upon Yamacraw Bluff, above the Savannah River, and some eighteen miles from the sea. A city of grace and enveloping serenity, it offers shaded streets, scarred and vine-covered walls, aging and crumbling façades, old houses, new houses, elegant houses. There are many churches, one of which lets loose with its chimes on Sunday mornings along Bull Street, a wide thoroughfare of out-of-this-world tranquillity, and there is the fearsome daily tolling of the great bell in the Cathedral of St. John the Baptist.

There have been, and there are, ugly and slum-stricken areas in this river port of incommunicable beauty, and perhaps it's more than a little ironical that the city's large-scale red-light district used to flourish upon the avenue bearing the name of the city's founder. Savannah had its beginning with the arrival of General James Edward Oglethorpe in 1733.

Savannah, for all of its expansion and industrial development and notwithstanding the discontinuance, more or less, of the 2 P.M. siestas for businessmen, is a city that has remained seemingly unchanged. It is still cleaved by the solemnly beautiful Bull Street; it is still a city of azaleas, oleanders, and magnolia trees; still blissfully unaware of any restrictions against the sale of alcohol. Savannah, pride of the uninhibited county of Chatham, was seemingly never told that such a thing as prohibition ever existed.

I was born in a formidable three-story house, grim and gray-yellow, at the intersection of Jones and Habersham Streets. An enormous oak gave shade to the corner, trolley cars screeched and clattered along the Habersham tracks. Horse-drawn ice wagons, selling great blocks of ice for ten cents, were forever pausing at the Jones Street curb, and wailing oyster women, with their burdens balanced securely upon their heads, called out their wares during all daylight hours.

Those ice wagons and the melancholy cries of the vendor-women have stayed in my memory, along with the displays of pies in the Schwartz bakery, the gigantic ice-cream sodas at the Solomon drugstore, the penny candies at Mr. Murphy's small and narrow store in Liberty Street, the open trolleys that made the trip to Isle of Hope, the magnolia trees and the chinaberries, the rattling train ride to Tybee Island, the barrels of lemonade at the Sunday-school picnics, and the great

23

street bonfire that was always in our block on Christmas night

In my growing-up years I had the thrill of riding several times in an automobile, the sedate electric that belonged to the family physician, Dr. Daniel. I sometimes sold candy between acts at the matinees at the Savannah Theater for the privilege of seeing the plays and did the same at the Vanderbilt Cup Races, which brought such sensational drivers as Ralph De Palma and Louis Wagner and Nazarro and Louis Chevrolet into the competition and which had such cars as the Benz, the Fiat, the Mercedes, the Lancia, the Lozier, and the Buick whirling over a fast and dangerous course. I played baseball in the squares, particularly in those along Abercorn and Habersham Streets; went many times to the Union Station to watch the backing in of the trains for the North, on their way up from Florida, and to listen to the booming and station-shaking voice of the train announcer as he called off the magic names of the cities that lay on the route.

I had a bicycle, of course, and tragedy came into my life when I lost it one afternoon at the Savannah baseball park, after I had found a fine peephole to watch the game between Savannah's South Atlantic League professionals and the team from Augusta, the club that sent Ty Cobb to Detroit. I had skates, as almost all the boys I knew did, but instead of going with them to the long paved stretches of the Park Extension, I did most of my skating along the rough sidewalk of Jones Street in the hope of catching the attention of Katharine Sutcliffe or Ulita Fernandez, who had luxuriant dark hair and beautiful eyes and made many trips to the North, always writing me long pen-and-ink letters from Simonson Avenue, Staten Island.

I'm certain that the fact that I wore eyeglasses saved me from many slappings and beatings, but they also contributed to at least one victory. In one of those I'll-see-you-right-after-school encounters my antagonist was a taller and stronger boy named David Hirsch. In taking his first swing at me, a roundhouse right, he grazed my face and sent my glasses spinning. They flew against a brick wall and were shattered. David was so unnerved by this incident and by the thought of having to replace them, as predicted in the shrieks of a ring of spectators, that he lost all of his demoniacal urge and I knocked him flat with a blow to the jaw. To my relief and astonishment he rose and dashed off down Lincoln Street and I was formally proclaimed the winner. I can't recall whether such a thing ever happened again.

I was wearing glasses by the time I was four or five—so ordered by the celebrated specialist, Dr. Calhoun of Atlanta, who performed a serious operation. He gave my parents the distressing news that I would have to go along for the rest of my life with only 5 per cent vision in one eye, but with normal vision in the other—with glasses. I've always wanted to believe that imperfections of eyesight accounted, to some extent, for the fact that I was an atrocious scholar in mathematics.

My father, Augustus Ward Morehouse, born in Screven County, Georgia, and the son of the Reverend Norman David Morehouse, who went into the South from Kent, Connecticut, attended Georgia's Emory College for two years, and was in wholesale groceries in Thomasville, Georgia, before starting out in Savannah in 1893 in the baking-powder business. He later turned to the manufacture of lumber. He was a man with a lively interest in civic affairs and he was also a joiner—the Kiwanis, the TPA, the Board of Trade, the Building Exchange. He served for some time as president of the Savannah Fair and once ran for mayor. He accepted defeat with commendable gallantry and he seemed to be talking from the heart when he told family and friends that he was glad he did not win—that his responsibilities in business, along with the happy hours that fishing afforded him, were quite sufficient to keep him busy for the rest of his days.

His love of fishing was something inherited from his own father. He was scornful of salt-water fishing and had no interest at all in the big-game variety and its elaborate and organized procedure. He just liked to find a good fresh-water stream —his favorite river was the Ogeechee—and sit for hours upon its bank with pole and line, using earthworms for bait. The particularly lively ones delighted him, and he was deft in putting them upon his hooks. There would be times when he would remain for half a day without getting a bite, but when the rain came—and he seemed to have a way of producing it in the late afternoon—those Ogeechee fish got hungry. My younger brother and I accepted his invitations to the river eagerly, got bored during the inactivity, and longed to go back to town, but when father's cork began bobbing during a downpour we found ourselves sharing his great excitement. I've never seen a happier man than A. W. M. was when he came up with a big, fighting, red-bellied perch, and there was something positively eloquent in his disgust when his pole, after being bent double, produced only an oversized eel or a gigantic mudcat.

Augustus Ward Morehouse, short and compact, was a man of humor, gentleness, and, on occasion, stubbornness. He was given to neatness in dress, liked white tropical suits, was never without his diamond stickpin, and his thin gold watch was attached to a gold chain strung across his waistcoat. He wore felt hats during the winter, straws in the summer, and regarded a good shoeshine as a sound business investment. He made frequent trips to Atlanta and to Baltimore in connection with his business, was never beyond the borders of the United States, and on his only trip to California he removed his well-polished shoes when he came to a strip of beach and went wading in the Pacific. I recall the elation with which he told my mother about it immediately after his return to Savannah. I never knew of my father taking a drink of liquor—alcoholic beverages were never served in our house—but he liked his chew of tobacco and an occasional cigar. He was a churchman, being a member of the Wesley Monumental, and he and my mother were in the family pew, third row from the front on the right, unfailingly every Sunday. He was devoted to his church and considered churchgoing an important part of his life, but he was never upset by my resistance to services as my mother was.

A careful and extraordinarily conservative man, my father considered it his duty to answer every letter that reached his desk, and he was forever urging my mother to have her charge-account bills paid by the tenth of each month and thus take advantage of the 10 per cent discount allowed by department stores and numerous business concerns of Savannah. He was scrupulously honest and expected the same from everyone. He was flabbergasted when he discovered that one of his trusted and long-term employees, a man he respected and genuinely liked, had been systematically stealing company funds for years. When his anger subsided he was overcome with distress, and at home late one afternoon he remarked, "I just don't see any good of being in business at all." He did not prosecute the embezzler; there were tears in his eyes when he dismissed him from the company's service.

My father wasn't given to tirades. His eruptions came infrequently, but he did speak often of the value of a man telling the truth. When I was twelve years old a policeman on the Habersham Street beat broke up a ball game we were having on the square. There were shouts of derision from some of the group when they felt they were at a safe distance. The policeman gave chase, overtook two of us, and told me I was under arrest for cursing the law. That evening, after hours of great tumult, my father came to me and said, "Son, I just want to know one thing. Did you swear at that cop? Did you use profanity? Did you call him a damned old fat-bellied, flat-footed bluecoat?" I told my father that I didn't, that at least twelve boys would say that I didn't utter a word. He went to police headquarters and had the hearing of my case deferred, took time out from his business to call upon each of the twelve boys whose names I gave him, and two days later produced them all in court. One by one, the twelve took the stand and gave their rehearsed testimony. Perhaps, ruled the recorder indulgently, the officer was just a bit mistaken about the boy who had done the cursing; there were *three* boys, not just one, in our group wearing glasses, and it was just possible that Patrolman Cohen had arrested the wrong ballplayer. The case was dismissed. My father, his victory won, returned to the affairs of the Morehouse Manufacturing Company.

I grew up in a family of five children—three girls and two boys. My older sister, Miriam, was a brilliant student in high school and at Wesleyan College, and she had definite talent as a painter, but she was frail and sickly throughout her life. Her code during her youth was "to have a date every night or you were finished," and there were callers at our house in an unending procession.

My two younger sisters were Sara and Elizabeth, whom we called Dolly. In her growing-up years Dolly's beaux were around the house in layers. Dolly was as pretty as any of those lovely Perkins girls, who lived in the big house just down the block in Henry Street. Pretty and blondish and impulsive and generous, with stage yearnings but without talent of any kind, she was a directionless person and what she needed was what my mother called a "good marriage." But she didn't get it in two tries. She became confused, reckless, and frantic; her life was actually over before she was thirty. I had been living in New York for some ten years when there came a call from the police at 2 A.M. saying that a young woman thought to be Elizabeth Morehouse of Savannah, Georgia, had been found dead in a small hotel in the Thirties. I went to the City Morgue and made the identification. Dolly, bored with her life at home, confused, unhappy, and always reaching out for the unachievable, had come on to New York with some vague idea of getting work. To the North by bus and, a few days later, back to Georgia in a coffin aboard the *Havana Special*.

My sister Sara was—and is—a remarkable person. A woman without poise but completely without pose—unaffected, outspoken, earthy, and genuinely good. She married her girlhood sweetheart upon his graduation from the Naval Academy, and excitedly took up the life of a Navy wife, liking it, relishing it, freely giving out her warmth and her friendship, and living with him in Annapolis, in Newport, in China, in Hawaii, and bearing him two beautiful children. They were stationed in Hawaii for many months and, like so many others of the American naval colony, forever sensed inevitable warfare with the Japs. Sara and the children were evacuated to San Francisco just prior to the Pearl Harbor tragedy. Her husband survived the horror of that catastrophe and, along with numerous classmates, gave prayer for more action and fitting retaliation. On Sunday afternoon, November 15, 1942, at exactly 5:45 o'clock, there was a doorbell ring at Sara's house in Coronado, California. She opened the door; two young Western Union messengers were on the porch. They just looked at her and stared. Sara was seized with terrible premonition as she gazed into their eyes. Finally, the larger boy blurted out, "Are you alone, lady? You will need somebody here when you open this." Then he handed her a two-star telegram which read, "The Navy Department deeply regrets to inform you that your husband, Louis Marcel Le Hardy, Lt. Comdr., USN, was killed in battle in the service of his country November 13,

1942, and was buried at sea with full military honors." Sara's eyes filled; she just stood there, quivering. The trees and houses across the street reeled around her. The two messengers began weeping and became hysterical. Recovering somewhat, Sara said, "I want to be alone. Please go." A few minutes later the Le Hardy children came in. Commander Le Hardy had gone to his death aboard the dauntless *San Francisco* as he and others of Admiral Callaghan's staff faced the enemy's attack from the bridge. Only one staff officer escaped slaughter in that fierce exchange of fire.

Sara, after telling her children, called my mother in Savannah. She received the news with her usual and extraordinary courage. Some months later she got word that her grandson, Morehouse Bowyer, my sister Miriam's boy, had suffered critical burns and facial mutilation in the crash of a RAF bomber. Mosey, as we called him, made his way to England via a freighter, serving as a cook, because he just couldn't stay out of the war. Many months of treatment in a plastic-surgery hospital followed—operation after operation to restore features, operations that would have made him unrecognizable to all of those who had known him prior to his crash. Finally, with only half a face, he entered Cambridge University, and there he died.

That news was also given my mother via the telephone at 1127 Henry Street. Tragedy, so often in her life, never brought on any breaking of her spirit, any lessening of her great belief in God, any diminution in her love of her religion. An indomitable woman, Sallie McIntosh Morehouse, who had zest for living, a capacity for helpfulness and good will, and who retained her courage, her faith, her humor, her cheerfulness until she was in the mid-eighties; even during the last year of her life, one accompanied by injury and pain and blindness, she was uncomplaining and unafraid.

My mother was a woman with a passion for neatness, a quality reflected in her dress, her housekeeping, her plan of life. When she reached seventy-five she began talking of the end of her years; she said that most of the Morehouses lived long, but that she knew her time was nearing its close, and she had very definite ideas as to how she wanted her funeral handled and the flowers arranged in the family plot in Bonaventure Cemetery, which she loved as she did her church. "I want to die in order," she often remarked. She was remarkably direct in her approach to all problems. When told by her doctor, a year or so before her death, that a serious operation was necessary, she considered the matter judicially.

"All right," she said, "I can go through with it—I've gone through with more than that—but first I have a question I must ask Mr. Clark at the bank." She got my brother Norman to drive her to the Liberty National Bank and Trust Company offices, took a chair beside the desk of the vice-president and trust officer, and said, "I want the truth. Can the estate really afford this operation? If we have the money, all right. Otherwise, I'm sure I'd die right there on the operating table."

Sallie Morehouse, throughout her years, and for months after her vision was greatly impaired, always remembered the birthdays of her children, nieces and nephews, and others of her kin with notes enclosing checks. Her notes were unfailingly cheerful, regardless of circumstances at the moment of the writing. She never put a line or a word into a letter that would disturb the recipient. She was a sentimentalist, with a touch of the eccentric at times. My father admired her auburn hair; she kept it dyed for him during the final years of his life. She was past eighty when she gave a dinner party for children and grandchildren at a restaurant on the outskirts of Savannah, and as we all sat down she announced, "Everybody at this table knows how I disapprove of alcohol in any form. If anybody has a drink tonight I won't know it. I'm that close to being blind." She never failed to write "God bless you, my dear, precious boy" in every letter she ever sent to me, and I don't believe she ever went out of her house without wearing the water-color miniature of my father, painted half a century before. Her eyes always showed their tears when she spoke of him in the years following his death, and during the delirium of her final days she called to him often. In her last consciousness, as the nurse stood at her bedside, she cried, "Oh, Ward, I'm so glad you're here. . . . I've been trying to find you."

Those words were, I believe, the last that Sallie McIntosh Morehouse ever spoke.

My brother Norman displayed an early interest in machinery of every kind, in dogs and in livestock in general, but he gave up on goats completely after a goat that belonged to me —a scraggly and powerful animal that followed me about like a dog—took a running start and, with head down, rammed brother Norman with great violence against a brick wall. My father rendered a severe decision: we would get rid of the goat. But what of the shiny wagon and the very special set of new goat harness? My father thought it over and announced a verdict that somehow delighted me: I would sell the harness for whatever it might bring but I would retain the wagon and, for the period of a week, in compensation for giving up my pet goat, brother Norman would get between the shafts and pull me once a day around the block, or the equivalent distance in any given direction. Dictatorship in Jones Street. Norman accepted the mandate, but without humor or grace. He carried out the orders. He thus became known, in the immediate neighborhood, as "Nornie the Goat."

Kids were "playing Indian" in south Georgia in the century's early years, although it was not a world in which Hopalong Cassidy had created a place for himself. We all daubed on war paint and wore feathers and once, after capturing a terrified paleface by the name of George Griffin lurking near our back yard, we tied him to the stake and proceeded to get a fire going beneath him. His shrieks led to his release before his pants actually caught fire. The next day, when I incautiously ventured into his territory unaccompanied by members of my tribe, the young and badly scorched Mr. Griffin sprang upon me and gave me a terrific beating.

For all of my fascination with Indian lore and a longing for life on the great plains, I can still recall my acute misery upon being assigned to appear as a red, red Indian in a grammar-school pageant when I aspired to the heroic role of Christopher Columbus! Perhaps it was right then that I resolved to have an acting company of my own.

I read a great deal in my youth—Dickens, Sir Walter Scott, G. A. Henty, Mark Twain, Jack London, Horatio Alger, the novels of McCutcheon and Chambers and David Graham

34

Phillips, and the five-cent thrillers—the *Liberty Boys of '76, Frank and Dick Merriwell, Old King Brady,* and *Young Wild West,* all of which had to be hidden from my parents. I went often to the public library to see the files of the *New York Herald* for news of the Broadway plays and spent many hours in the library at the high school reading, and almost memorizing, the play reviews of Mathew White, Jr., in *Munsey's Magazine.*

I went hunting Saturdays. I had a boyhood passion for guns, along with an inordinate appreciation of the romantic novels of the time, and often took a novel with me on expeditions into the nearby woods. I moved on from an air rifle to a .22 rifle to a single-barrel shotgun and eventually to a double-barrel, first with hammers and then hammerless. I never became involved in tragedy through use of firearms, but they did serve to provide some drama in my youth. One Saturday morning, with a brand-new gun, my Christmas present, I was heading for the rice fields when a big Negro came alongside me and said he would walk with me and show me more ricebirds than I'd ever seen in all my life. That pleased me greatly. But when we reached an isolated area, after another mile or so, he suddenly snatched my beautiful gun from my shoulder, fired a shell over my head, and told me to start running back to town or he would fill me full of birdshot. I began running—and weeping—and didn't stop until I had reached police headquarters.

And then there was the Christmas morning when a lanky, good-looking, and tomboyish girl named Louise Golden thrust a .22 pistol, loaded with a blank cartridge, against my cheek and said, "Don't you dare me to shoot because I will." "You won't do any such thing," I said, with the bravado of fourteen years. "Won't I?" she cried. And she pulled the trigger. I thought for the instant that my entire face had been blown away; I was certain that I was to be disfigured for life. The powder seared my flesh and left a black and bleeding circle larger than a silver dollar. Three months of treatment by a skin specialist and six months of massages at the most expensive beauty parlor were needed to remove most of the powder burn. A bluish smear remained for two years or so.

In teen-age years I came very close to making a home of the YMCA. Perhaps my great fondness for the Y can be attributed to the fact that I was the underwater champion in the swimming pool and that a stage was provided for putting on plays by my amateur group, known as the Minor Stock Company. We did many plays in Savannah and in nearby towns. My best actor was Donald Spann, who prudently retained his job in the bank notwithstanding my urging that he give it up and go in completely for the theater. Our leading woman, Julie Peck, blond and stocky, always listened when I pleaded with her to rush away to New York and give her rare talents a chance, but she wisely stayed where she was. Our ingenue, Catherine Coyle, went into a dead faint when we rehearsed her until 2 A.M., but she was back for more rehearsing the next day. We had our triumphs, with plays of my own writing and with those we got from Samuel French and with those we "adapted" from road productions on-from-Broadway that played the famous old Savannah Theater, fronting on Bull Street and Chippewa Square. We went to the town of Clyo with a drama, *Down in the Deep South,* auctioned off a five-pound box of cheap candy between the acts, and the next morning, at daybreak, counted out the intake, $66 in silver and currency, on the cold bare floor. Our funniest play, *The Little Red Mare,* the sure-fire laugh producer in the repertoire, was selected as the play to be given at the town hall at Millen; we played it without a slip, but there wasn't so much as one audible giggle from the audience. Later, when we went nervously to the sponsor to collect our share of the receipts, he told us not to worry. The play went all right. The people in Millen were just a little odd: they never laughed at anything.

Our Minor Stock Company gave Eugene Walter's *Paid in Full,* or an approximation of it, on a creaky stage built in my back yard. Donald Spann was the carpenter, electrician, and mechanical genius in our organization and had told me not to touch the lumber, nails, hammer, shovel, and saw which he had carefully assembled; he was going to South Carolina for a two-week summertime visit and would put up the stage immediately upon his return. It would be up to me to get the script into shape for rehearsal. But on one of those 99-degrees-in-the-shade mornings, as I was fumbling with Donald's tools upon the site selected for our platform, I noticed that I had a spectator—a pretty girl, unsmiling and motionless, was gazing down from the third-story porch next door. Her arms were upon the railing; she just stood there, staring. Deciding to watch her and without appearing to do so, I began to get busy and dug a hole for one of the log chunks obtained by Donald for a platform support. I got it firmly into the ground, took a quick look to make sure that I had retained my audience, and

37

then I went in for a bit of sawing, as awkwardly as possible, and did some more digging for the posts. Every morning for about ten days I returned to the job; every day, as my hammering began, the girl next door would appear at the railing and remain transfixed until my labors were done. She never spoke; she never smiled; there was never any exchange of greeting, but she was a faithful and inspirational watcher. When Donald Spann got back from the country he reported at my house for the big construction job. He was incredulous when he found the stage all in place and ready for the actors. He decided that it was wobbly but serviceable; he congratulated me with a fervor that somehow exceeded his enthusiasm for my performance in *The Little Red Mare* or in *The Fortune Hunter*. "Doggone it," he said, "I think it's wonderful, but I still can't understand why you did it or how you did it. I didn't think you even knew how to drive a nail."

Well, we gave *Paid in Full* upon that stage and before an audience that included James H. Doyle, the famous stock-company director. He immediately offered Donald and myself small parts in the Schiller Players' production of *Brewster's Millions*. I played an office boy who got hurled through a second-act doorway and also joined the backstage crew in helping with the storm-at-sea effects during the third-act shipwreck scene. Another chance with the professionals came when the handsome and buxom and competent Henrietta Brown, stock star, put us into a week's presentation of the Paul Armstrong melodrama, *Alias Jimmy Valentine*. Florence Olmstead later told me that my performance of Dick the Rat was quite as much of a work of art as any performance I'd ever given in her classes in ancient history. In history I was as good as I was deplorable in mathematics.

I went along with my schooling, faring well in the subjects I liked, and enduring humiliation from B. F. Pickett, the high-school principal, who also taught geometry. He was a tyrant, a bellowing bear of a man, who appeared to take a positive relish in berating those who were mystified by mathematics. I'm sure that I despised him; I'm also sure that I was deeply in love with the ethereal Florence Olmstead and was forever under the spell of the pretty Julia Boyle, my out-of-school art teacher, whose good looks held the interest of a fairly ruffianly group when her instructions in charcoal, pen and ink, water color, and pastels did not. I was no whirlwind in Latin but was some-how fascinated by Mrs. Strong, a woman of severity, dignity, humor, and humanity, who taught it.

Interesting friends and neighbors from teen-age years remain, of course, in the memory of all of us. In my case, there was Katharine Sutcliffe, who lived in the next block and who had beautiful golden curls, a bewitching smile, and toothpick legs. She was, I'm sure, my first formal "date," going with me to the tiny cinema theater called the Superba in Bull Street and then having ice cream at Conida's next door, an afternoon's outing that called for an expenditure of a quarter, inclusive of a five-cent sack of chocolates. Katharine moved away from Jones Street just as she was getting to be known as "Ward's girl," and a romance of adolescence was unceremoniously blasted.

A lazy, long-legged boy, Carl D. Stults, with a spot of white in his hair, was always the object of my respect and affection.

He was fairly agonizing to the enchanting Florence Olmstead, showing no interest at all in the heroics of Carthage or the rise and fall of the Roman Empire, but he was uncommonly gifted in Latin and he was the best teen-age bird shot in all of Chatham County. His proficiency with the shotgun has remained with him through the years. In our occasional expeditions in the broom sage in quest of bobwhite quail we still talk of the time we shot six guinea hens belonging to a Chatham County farmer and of how our Christmas was almost ruined when he called at our respective homes and angrily demanded payment at the rate of ten dollars per hen. He eventually settled for five dollars.

I had my woes with arithmetic while attending grade school —Massie School, an aging structure with cracked and yellowing plaster, located in Gordon Street—and I was fairly miserable with my struggles with algebra and geometry after graduating into high school. During a geometry examination, midway in my junior year, Professor Pickett came alongside my desk and found me engaged in the writing of the second act of a play called *Mr. Doom Gets a Letter* and he berated me so severely I left my desk, left the room, and was done with the Savannah High School forever. That afternoon, at football practice—I'd decided to have a go at it for one last day—I was told by the class team coach, the dark, stubby Cy Span, quarterback on the varsity team and the best kicker on the squad, that I'd made the team as right end. "Too late," I said. "I'm taking a job tomorrow with the Central of Georgia Railroad."

For a period of three months or so I complicated the affairs

of the Central of Georgia considerably, without actually creating any train wrecks, but quit that job in a hurry when Donald
Spann, my stand-by in the operation of the Minor Stock Company, came along with an offer for our company to appear in
the big auditorium of Benedictine College, on a fifty-fifty
basis. We'd long yearned to be seen at Benedictine College
and we liked doing plays under the sponsorship of Catholic
societies; they always sold tickets and gave us packed houses.
And it was a capacity audience that greeted our presentation
of Eugene Walter's melodrama of the Canadian wilds, *The
Wolf*. There was a six-inch layer of leaves from sycamore
trees upon the stage to give realism to a forest scene when the
play started, and the audience responded with sustained applause. I appeared as the play's hero, a French-Canadian, and
Donald Spann was the villain in the role of an American
engineer. The script called for a tussle in the dark in the final
act, and Spann and I went about it with such ferocity that
my knife blade penetrated his abdomen. He was bleeding
freely when he took his bow at the final curtain.

By this time, at the age of sixteen, I'd written twenty plays,
most of which had been staged by the Minor Stock Company
and the twenty-first, to come along later, and called *His Own
Home Town*, was given presentation upon the stage of the
Savannah Theater, the famous playhouse in which all the
touring companies appeared, and which had been our company's objective for many months. In the fall of 1913 the
Minor Stock Company's activities were abruptly suspended
as I was packed off for Dahlonega and the North Georgia
Agricultural College (the "Agricultural" was later dropped

from the name), a school of my father's choice. He averred that it was a "sensible" selection and dismissed, as gross extravagance, my notion of wanting to attend the New Mexico Military Institute in faraway Roswell. He was not a man given to tirades, to holding forth, but my repeated efforts to get New Mexico into the mealtime conversation precipitated a Sunday dinner outburst, during which he remarked that it took an awful lot of hard work to raise and provide for a family, and that we all seemed to think that he was made of money. He rose and left the table without tasting the homemade banana ice cream, his favorite dessert. Our meal was finished in silence.

But in the end, Dahlonega appealed to me. I liked its remoteness and inaccessibility—a gold-mining town, 25 miles from the railroad at Gainesville, and high in the Blue Ridge Mountains. I'd never seen a mountain until I got to Lumpkin County. I liked the air, the morning mists in the red-clay country. Weighing less than 120 pounds in those days, I enjoyed the hill climbing and the hikes into the mountainous areas, but it was my slightness that kept me off the football team, notwithstanding the fact that my flying-tackle technique, brought on by impromptu football in Savannah's sand lots, parks, and squares, had won the attention of the head coach in scrimmages between the varsity and the eager, willing, desperate nonvarsity multitude. Perhaps it was just as well that I was too light to make the varsity squad because there came the day when the Riverside Military Academy, on from Gainesville, turned loose a thunderbolt of a halfback named Hickman. He ran for six touchdowns and left bruised and incautious Dahlonega tacklers strewn the length of the field.

My 120 pounds didn't help me greatly in fist fights during the first two or three months of being "off at school." The college mail was brought over from Gainesville in horse-drawn hacks—sections of the road were red-clay quagmires and few automobiles of the day could get through without floundering —and it was distributed by the school's mailman who took up his stand on the same spot of the campus around four o'clock every afternoon and screamed out the names of the recipients as he snatched the mail from his big leather bag, letter by letter. I got a lot of mail—undoubtedly because I wrote more letters than anybody at the NGAC—and during the mail-call sessions there was the call, "Morehouse!" several times, and always with the result there would be a chorus of cries, "Morehouse! Poorhouse! Outhouse!" And, for variations, the hecklers even got around to "Whorehouse." I didn't like it; I got mad, and I fought. I caught one fellow student as he yelled and hit him squarely on the jaw. He spun around, half fell, and then knocked me flat. Every day, and for week upon week, I tried to flatten my tormentors and, in consequence, went around with a more or less permanent set of black eyes. Finally, after I'd slugged and had been slugged until well past Thanksgiving, a student leader came up to me during a mail call, put his hand on my shoulder, and turned to the group milling about the mailman. "Listen now, you fellows. Cut it out. This boy can't lick the whole school. From now on his name is Morehouse—and that's all." So it was thereafter.

A military school, North Georgia College had a curriculum

on the level with the state university at Athens, and I enjoyed my year and a half there. I·drilled with Company A, carried a rifle, made the sharpshooter team, and got my face slapped by Rea Meaders, the prettiest girl in town, for trying to kiss her (as directed in the script) during the rehearsal of a school play. I enjoyed the philosophy of a farm-boy roommate named Jubal Cox, a great hulk of a youth who made guard on the football squad, I became Memorial Day speaker at the exercises in the auditorium, and found an understanding friend in the English professor, George W. Camp. Perhaps he blinked a bit when he came upon a one-act play, which I had turned in instead of a treatise on Milton's *Paradise Lost*. But he said that he had enjoyed reading *The Man Who Owned the Blue Ridge* and thought that it might have more commercial value than any Miltonian essay I could have written.

Several months after I returned to Savannah, leaving Dahlonega at the midterm because I wanted to try to take up the theater professionally, my father said that he was ready for a long talk with me and I was fairly terrified by the thought of it. I had never been at ease in his presence, or he in mine. I had gone through my boyhood actually avoiding him and had come to know that while my mother was likely to grant any request, to indulge any whim, to give me money from her own savings when I wanted a new bicycle or a new gun or ammunition for an old one, my father was always certain to consider pleas for extra money judicially. I was certainly aware that I respected him for his civic-mindedness, for his insistence upon paying all bills on time, and for his standing in the com-

44

munity. I was also quite conscious of his conservatism and rebelled against it. There was bitter disappointment in my heart when we had failed to move from Henry Street into a beautiful house on Victory Drive, after due announcement had been made in the press. My father, upon thinking it over, had decided that the cost was too much, that the Henry Street house was comfortable enough, that the money was needed for other things. My desolation then was comparable to the envy that had come upon me in the dormitory at Dahlonega when I stepped across the hall and into the room shared by the dark and dapper Casey Jones of Rome, Georgia, and the flamboyant Carrio Williams from Jacksonville, Florida. Their room was a riot of pennants, flage, photographs—softly lighted, richly carpeted, and walls done in pagoda red.

When my father remarked, toward the end of a meal, that he wanted to talk with me, and immediately, I began wondering what I'd done at Dahlonega that had brought forth a protest from north Georgia. I left my dessert untouched and went tremblingly to the upstairs bedroom which he and my mother occupied—they shared a double bed throughout their long married life—and sat down and waited for the ordeal to begin. He paced the room, adjusted his spectacles, turned to me and said abruptly, "Ward, I'm going to offer you a place in my business." He then motioned for silence and went along with his talk. He was willing to forget that I had cost his company a thousand-dollar order, during summertime fill-in work at his office, because I had told the prospective customer to call back the next day, that nobody else was around, and that I was then engaged in the writing of the climactic scene of a second act.

"We'll put that down to inexperience and not to genius," my father said, and then he went on to tell me that he was willing to dismiss a valued employee to make room for me if I'd promise to forget the stage and settle down to business. He was even willing to start me at what seemed an extraordinary wage, $15 weekly. He was giving me, as he saw it, my great chance.

We were together for an hour. Finally, I muttered something about being pleased and grateful, and asked for a little time to think it over. It was all very fine of him and I was flattered by his confidence, but I wasn't sure that I wanted a business career. I wasn't sure at all.

"Well," he said, looking at me steadily, "if you don't take this what will you do? Play Hamlet? Play Shakespeare and starve?"

"I would like to be a playwright," I said. "I received a letter from John Craig of the Castle Square Theater in Boston telling me that *His Own Home Town* has great promise. Besides writing plays, I'd like to travel. . . ."

"Impractical nonsense," he said.

"Perhaps it is, but will you give me a few days to make up my mind? Will you give me a week?"

"All right," he said. "Take a week. Take two weeks."

A few days later a telegram arrived from Asheville, North Carolina. It was the telegram that I had been expecting.

## chapter three

~~~~~~~~~~~~~

CHARLES RICHMOND had an aquiline nose and long, thick black hair that curled obediently about his neck. His eyes were mild blue, his voice sonorous, his manner that of a grand-style tragedian, and there was something of an elegance, along with a certain seediness, in his dress. He was lean and gaunt and about 5 feet 10; he had high cheekbones, somewhat overlarge ears, and arms that seemed longer than they actually were.

He was an itinerant professional reader, specializing in Shakespeare, and he was letter-perfect in the rantings of King Lear, the broodings of Macbeth, the cackling of Justice Shallow, and in the hearty speech of the swaggering Petruchio. My friend Richmond was a man of undetermined years— probably in his early sixties. He had been an actor of sorts, playing numerous engagements in character roles with resident stock companies that were scattered throughout America in the years of 1910–1915 and he was, as I came to know him, the star of his own one-man show—his own manager, his own advance man, his own booking agent, and his own secretary. There were no lecture bureaus operating in the South during the first decade of this century, and the infrequent Shakespearean presentations in the larger cities were made only when the companies of the established road stars, such as Robert Mantell, E. H. Sothern, and John E. Kellerd, ventured below the Rappahannock.

Charles Richmond carried photographs, letterheads, personal cards, testimonials, and press clippings—his bag was his filing cabinet, and there were always stray clippings in a pocket of his shiny blue suit—and he did manage to arrange some of his appearances by advance correspondence, but his touring was generally impromptu. He would set out from New York in some general direction, never certain of his itinerary. He preferred to visit towns of 20,000 and less, and he frequently decided upon a stopover because he liked the name of the place, or because it had something about it that appealed to him. He once told me that he went to the city of Danville, Virginia, only because he wanted to see the river Dan, and that he put Savannah, Georgia, on his route after he had heard of the beauty of its gigantic, aging live oaks, festooned with clusters of gray moss.

Richmond would generally arrive in a city unheralded and unheeded, this being due to the informality of his tours, the flexibility of his schedule, and the swiftness and suddenness of his changes of mood and mind. He would work out an engagement and work up an audience after he had found himself a hotel or a boardinghouse. He seldom made an appearance in the regular road playhouse of a town or city along his course—its stage was probably taken over by a touring company of *St. Elmo* or *McFadden's Flats* or Dockstader's Minstrels at the time of his arrival. He preferred lodge auditoriums. Never being too realistic about monetary returns, and generally satisfied with just enough to pay for a bed and meals and day-coach fare—he rode thousands of miles in his cross-country wanderings on the dusty red-plush seats of the grimy locals of his day—he was always glad to make an appearance in the study hall of a high school or in the school auditorium. He enjoyed himself most when he was doing his act before a small, select audience in the parlor or living room of a private home. Something of a vagabond and a mountebank, my friend Richmond, and he frequently had all of the glibness of a professional pitchman, but he was also a true artist. He was a student of Shakespeare; he had a love for the work he was doing. He was, therefore, notwithstanding the precariousness of his calling, a man of a certain invincibility. He made his living the hard way; he gave more than he got; he seldom failed to stimulate an audience and to satisfy himself with his own performance.

I first set eyes upon Richmond, and heard him, when he spoke before a portion of the student body of the Savannah High School, delivering passages from *Hamlet* (he deeply impressed us all with the "O, what a rogue and peasant slave am I" soliloquy) and *The Merchant of Venice* and turning, for an encore, to merrier sequences, reciting bits of *Much Ado about Nothing* and *A Midsummer Night's Dream*.

49

Richmond was a success in his first Savannah appearance. Three years passed before he came to our city for a second visit, and he then seemed older, wearier, a little shabbier, but there was still the old fire in his eyes when he struck out into Shakespeare's impassioned verse. At the time he returned I was in a state of youthful and tormenting indecision and restlessness. I had a definite urge to break away from my hometown environment, this seeming to be a necessary and immediate step, but I didn't know just how to go about it. Then, in mid-May of the year 1915, I read in one of our two local papers that Richmond was to reappear for an afternoon engagement. I got the notion at that very instant that he was the man who could help me, and I had a front-row seat at his reading. A few hours later I called upon him at his hotel.

He received me with elaborate courtesy and listened as I stammeringly told him why I had come. Perhaps he could use an assistant during his summertime travels? Perhaps he might want someone to play a scene with him sometime? He sat in a battered lobby rocker, fanning himself with a palmetto fan, his gaze ceilingward, but when I gropingly reached the end of my well-rehearsed speech and said I was certain my family would give me a little money to contribute to the expenses of the tour, he turned his eyes upon me. A half-smile crossed his haggard face. He put aside his fan, thrust his hand into his coat pocket, and drew out a small sack of hard candy—candy, coins, train schedules, and a small bunch of keys were carried in that pocket, along with his press clippings—offered me a piece, and then bade me move my chair a bit closer. He then gave me, ever so unctuously, a talk about the hardships of a professional's life, of the perils of the stage, and why he had turned to it early in life instead of taking up teaching or sheep-herding. He paused in his rambling discourse with dramatic suddenness, such as he had used in his soothing recitations from the wisdom of old Polonius, and then said, quite cheer-fully, and with a note of optimism that fairly stunned me, that he just might have a place for a bright young man and that he would keep me in mind. He carefully scribbled down my name and address.

Two weeks passed. Three. Then came that telegram from Asheville, North Carolina—collect. Richmond was inviting me to join him, suggesting that I come immediately, and bring along fifty or perhaps seventy-five dollars. My father frowned when he noticed that the wire had been sent collect. "Don't like that," he said. "Perhaps it was just a mistake," said my mother quickly. "I still don't like it," my father said. "Only irresponsible people send telegrams that are not prepaid." "Per-haps not irresponsible, dear," continued my mother valiantly, "just a little forgetful. Aren't actors like that?" She knew of my yearning to be on my way—she had resolutely supported me in my reluctance to become a box manufacturer—and the next evening I was aboard the sleeper for Asheville, occupying a pullman berth for the first time in my life.

Richmond greeted me eagerly in Asheville, took charge of the seventy-five dollars that I had brought along—he had be-come a celebrated guest at his hotel, notwithstanding the fact that his bill was overdue, his stay overlong, and his funds seemingly nonexistent—and we made something of a tri-umphant exit as we set forth in the horse-drawn carryall to the

51

railroad station. "Well, young man," he said, with one of those bursts of geniality that came upon him when he was in a communicable mood, "we're on our way. Our first stop will be Johnson City, Tennessee. Glorious days are before us."

They were hardly that, but there were no dull hours. No business, either, in Johnson City. We went on to Bristol, Virginia–Tennessee, that bustling state-line city, checked into the YMCA—Richmond preferred the Ys to boardinghouses or small, out-of-the-way hotels, saying that a man could get a good bath and a bit of religion for the same price if he wanted it—and I learned that my reader-friend was a disciplinarian, a humanitarian, something of a vegetarian, and a man with a remarkable memory. "I once played here," he told me, "in a touring company of *The Shepherd King* and I met a fellow named Mr. B. Said he owned a business college. Go and find it and see if you can get us an engagement." I went. There was a business college in Bristol and a Mr. B. was running it, but he had no recollection of C. R. He didn't think, either, that his students would be interested in Shakespeare—he doubted if more than a few of them had ever heard of Shakespeare—and they had a pretty busy schedule at the college. But if I wanted to bring my friend around just to say hello. . . . Well, I delivered Richmond and he was superb. He talked and Mr. B. listened and as he listened he weakened and when we walked out of the place we had an engagement for 11:30 A.M. the next day for a reading before the shorthand class. "I won't get fancy with these kids," beamed my friend, his inevitable umbrella under his arm, as we strolled back to the Y. "I'll just give them the elementary stuff—*Hamlet, Julius Caesar, Mac-*

*beth.* And you, boy"—sometimes I was "my dear boy" and at other times just "boy"—"you will sit in the last row as an interested spectator and when it's all over I'll look toward you and say, 'I wonder if that young man in the back seat will help us with a little collection.' Then you'll get up and try to get a contribution from everybody present." The reading went on as scheduled. The shorthand students were respectfully attentive, they applauded politely, and our collection brought in $17.90, the man named B. contributing a ten-dollar bill. "Not much, but we'll do better next time," was Richmond's comment. He believed it, too. Pride in his work was one factor necessary to his calling, optimism was another.

During our otherwise profitless stay in Bristol I got to know Richmond a good deal better. He had moments of vast good humor and others of great austerity. There were many periods of silence and meditation, but I was never given the feeling that he was concerned about the low state of our finances or the problems of tomorrow. For all of his more or less continuous insecurity, he was never a worrier. He had a lively interest in people and, with his courtly manner and ready speech, he charmed and fascinated train conductors, brakemen, station agents, bellboys. Also, upon occasion hotel managers, to whom he frequently spoke on the matter of extension of credit.

Richmond liked an occasional glass of beer, but I never knew of his taking a drink of liquor, and when I would go with him for his beers he would always suggest that I gorge myself upon the free lunch that was generally available in the better saloons of 1915. He didn't seem to believe in spending money on haircuts—he didn't get one during the time I was with him—but he did permit himself certain modest extravagances, such as five-cent cigars and good five-cent shines. He cared a great deal more about the condition of his shoes than he did about that of his clothing. He never failed to thank the bootblack or to compliment him upon the excellence of his job.

"Doesn't ever hurt," he frequently said to me, "to make a man feel more important to himself. It only takes a few words. There are a lot of ornery people, but also more decent ones than you might think."

Richmond frequently displayed temperament and temper. He gave me a slap and went into an angry oration when I fell asleep as I was holding the prompt book for his rehearsal of Malvolio in *Twelfth Night*, and on an evening after one of his better performances I discovered that there were certain privileges that went along with being the star of the show, and that these were to be respected. He ordered an ice-cream sundae as we got to the fountain of a Virginia store and then he left his seat to accept the tribute of a matron who had been in his audience and who was still, and quite definitely, under his spell. When he returned to the fountain his eyes fell upon *two* sundaes, gigantic and nut-covered. He glared at me and then he spoke, "You were invited in here to have an ice cream, a plain ice cream, and nobody said anything at all about your having a sundae. For God's sake, do you think we have money to throw away? I want to warn you, boy, that this sort of extravagance can lead only to a most damnable insolvency."

That was a side of Charles Richmond I quietly detested, but he had gentler moods and moments and I often felt that he liked me and had a genuine interest in me. "You must learn something from this experience," he would say. "You must also develop an appreciation for Shakespeare. It will help you. Suppose your children want to know about Mercutio and Iago and Timon of Athens. Be sure that you can tell them." He was always asking me as we sat in hotel lobbies—a great deal of his life must have been spent in lobbies, with his big chair always near a brass spittoon—and as we waited for street-cars and rode in the smoky and stifling day coaches, what I intended doing with my life. "You'll have to make up your mind," he would say, and then he would tell me that one of the most important things a man must learn is how to hustle for himself.

We went to a dozen towns in the states of Tennessee and Virginia. I seldom had an idle moment. One of my principal assignments was that of getting the money at the end of each reading. There were times when the passing-the-hat method was used, and at other times I would collect from the person sponsoring the engagement the sum that had been previously agreed upon. The receipts from each appearance were barely enough to pay for food and lodging and the railroad fare to the next town.

Besides being the treasurer—it was only for appearances' sake, as I always turned the money over to Mr. R. when we were out of the hall and around the corner—I had many other duties. I was the booking agent, calling upon schools, libraries, and lodges, and frequently making house-to-house calls.

"Boy," Richmond would say in one of our hotel lobby conferences, "you must realize that the job you're doing requires leg work as well as head work. We've got to get Shakespeare into the homes. We're not selling kitchen utensils, we're selling culture. You must ring some doorbells in the better residential districts, but never until you think that the head of the house has gone to the office. You will then call and tell the dear lady that you've heard she's interested in the classics and that you represent a famous reader who will be in her town for only a short time. You will then say—and you must be very tactful about this, too—that her prestige in the community will be increased by sponsorship of Mr. Richmond. You must not press her for an immediate decision. Just say that you will return the next day for her answer. When her husband comes home for dinner she will spring it on him and make him think it is something that he wanted all the time. In that way, my dear boy, we'll get some engagements." And in that way we did—a few.

People were genuinely moved by Richmond's recitations; he made Shakespeare colloquial and understandable. There was no radio in those days, the touring theatrical companies, as active as they were in roaming America from ocean to ocean, did not reach many of the smaller towns, and when Richmond came along, shaggy but commanding, he brought culture and erudition with him. His rating as a student and a classicist was never challenged; he was accepted as an enlightened man in his field. He was always particularly impressive in his private-home readings, and it was after he had delighted an audience in a living room in Pulaski, Virginia, that the hostess fluttered up to him and said: "Dear Mr. Richmond, you have enthralled us. You have given us something that we have needed—and shall treasure. You must pay us another visit very, very soon. When may we expect the honor of hearing you again?"

"Madame," replied C. R. with a courtly bow, "you overwhelm me. I don't know just when my schedule will permit my return to your hospitable midst, but perhaps you would like a little more of *Hamlet* right now." There was excited applause, and he went into Hamlet's address to the Players and finished with the "Alas, poor Yorick" sequence.

Instead of being elated as we walked away from the house Richmond was strangely subdued. He didn't speak until we were back at the hotel. "They liked me tonight," he said, "but I wasn't good. I didn't feel right. Now, boy, tell me what was the matter with my performance. You must try to become a critic."

The business of going into a strange town and asking people to pay their good money for such a commodity as an hour's reading from *Richard III* and *Much Ado about Nothing* from a man they had never seen and had never heard of wasn't easy work, and these booking-agent duties took up most of my time. When I wasn't thus engaged I was holding the script for my boss at his rehearsals, taking long walks with him, or calling on the local editor to give the news of our arrival.

"What's wrong with the world, boy?" Richmond once asked as I proudly showed him a three-paragraph story which had appeared in the daily of a small Virginia town after I had visited the newspaper office. "Isn't there any culture left? Didn't anybody ever hear of Shakespeare—or of Booth and Barrett? Three paragraphs! There was a minstrel show through

57

here last week that got a whole column on the front page. The next time we come to this town I'm going to black up!"

A man of many hours of solitude throughout his life, Richmond never liked to dine alone. My presence at the evening meal was more or less compulsory and he made an event of it, regardless of whether we were perched on stools in a lunch stand or having dinner in a moderate-priced hotel. "Not the Waldorf-Astoria, boy," he would say when the state of our finances sent us into a lunch counter, "but we'll enjoy it. We'll do better tomorrow."

He was particularly voluble at dinnertime, and on the evening that we went to a Chinese restaurant he talked fascinatingly of his career in the theater, telling me how he got a job with Mantell and how he had lost one with Richard Mansfield. Suddenly, he stopped talking. His eyes were upon the check. "Boy," he said, "we can never pay for this wonderful meal and buy tickets on that train tomorrow." Just at this moment the smiling proprietor came along and asked if we had enjoyed our meal. Richmond, a man equal to almost any emergency, said that it had been the best Chinese dinner he had ever had, then asked Mr. Lum Lee Fung if he hadn't been born in Peiping. No, his birthplace was San Francisco, but his parents were from Peiping. Did Mr. R. know Peiping? Did he! My friend went into a ten-minute discourse on the charms and glories of that ancient city. When he finished the beaming and gratified restaurant man reached over and picked up the check. It would be his pleasure, he said, to have us as his guests.

On the way back to the hotel I said: "You have never

spoken of Peiping, Mr. Richmond. Did you go there as an actor?" "My boy," he said, "a little imagination now and then never hurt anybody. I was never in China in my life!"

We spent nearly three weeks in getting from Bristol to Roanoke. Three futile days in Wytheville, and I shall always remember it because of the elaborate and all-inclusive dinner served at the hotel for twenty-five cents. When we reached Christiansburg our funds were disturbingly low, and I recall having to walk a mile or so in the 90-degree heat from the railroad station to the town, and then walking back to the station. It was on the station platform, when we were a few cents shy of the fare to Roanoke, that Richmond's eyes suddenly brightened when he saw a familiar face. He strode over and shook hands with a priest he had known for years. The good Father let Richmond have three dollars. "Do you know why I was able to borrow that money, boy?" asked Richmond, as we sat in the waiting room. "It's because of a similar circumstance in Charleston, South Carolina, several years ago—and I paid him back. I always pay them back." We were soon in a crowded day coach on our way to the conquest of Roanoke, and we made the trip standing. Richmond had risen, with a sweeping bow, and had given our red-plush seat to a woman with a small boy.

Roanoke was fairly hospitable, giving us a reading at the BPOE hall and another in a private home in the suburbs, but after we had been there for a week—I found a room at a boardinghouse, which included meals, for four dollars weekly and he lived at the YMCA—we were again just about broke. My friend said we'd have to have a talk and he seemed actually

59

discouraged for the first time. We went into the park and sat on a bench. It was a hot night and I remember that his high, starched collar was wilting and a little soiled. He seemed suddenly older. He spoke to me in fatherly fashion, and without histrionics.

"Boy," he said, with deliberation, "we're not making out very well. I have just enough money left to buy a ticket to Lynchburg and I'm going there tomorrow morning on the first train. I know some good people in Lynchburg. I think I can get work immediately. If I do, I'll send for you and we'll go on up into New England—into Maine and Vermont. That's where the money is this time of the year. . . . Here's a dollar. That's all I can spare. Now you rustle for yourself and perhaps you can join me within a week. You'll hear from me." He rose, patted me on the head, and strode away, walking slowly. I watched him until he was out of the park.

So there I was, stranded. It was a new experience. A long way from home, with only sixty-eight cents besides Richmond's dollar, and I owed a week's board. My first thought was to send a telegram to Georgia. I could imagine the scene in Savannah upon the arrival of my wire—my father shaking his head, my brother laughing a little sardonically, my mother being upset and hurrying at once to the telegraph office. I sat there in the park for more than an hour, thinking it over and I decided against asking for help. If I was ever to achieve an independence, this was the test. There would be no distress signals from Roanoke; the time to begin rustling for myself had arrived. I went cheerfully back to my boardinghouse and, before going to bed, wrote my mother saying that Mr. R. and

I were doing well in Roanoke and would be staying for a while.

Two days later, after failing to get work with a visiting carnival or with the stock company playing at Roanoke's then famous Academy of Music, I gave up art and found a job with the Norfolk & Western Railroad at $35 a month, which seemed like a fortune. A week after I had reported at the N & W offices I received a letter from Richmond, addressed to me in care of General Delivery. He was still in Lynchburg. He wrote, "Sorry, boy, but I cannot ask you to join me just now. I didn't have the luck here that I expected and am going to Washington to try and get a place with the Poli stock company. You've got a lot of sense and you will make out. Keep rustling. You will hear from me."

During the rest of the summer, during the broiling months of July and August of 1915, I stayed in the employ of the N & W. In the evenings I worked on a play and read Shakespeare, always keeping in mind Richmond's scornful words about young people he had known who wasted their time. I was certain that he had gone out of my life completely but my thoughts were continually going back to our strange month-long partnership and to the vivid impressions that it had left with me—the rapt faces of the business-college students when he thunderingly reminded them that he came to bury Caesar and not to praise him; the tears that suddenly welled in the eyes of a one-armed pencil peddler when C. R. handed him a half dollar, took a pencil, and walked quickly away; the sudden panic that overcame my friend when he left the hotel in Wytheville without his umbrella—it was a sunny day—and returned hastily to get it. He explained that he had once been caught in a cloudburst in Kokomo, Indiana, and had come down with pneumonia. Since that time an umbrella had been a part of his day-to-day equipment. And he never returned to the state of Indiana.

In early September, after saving enough from my N & W earnings to buy a new suit and a railroad ticket, I returned to Savannah. It was something of a triumphant home-coming. My friends said it must have been pretty wonderful going to all those places, and I agreed that it certainly was. They began asking if I intended rejoining that Shakespearean fellow—or what? My father, obviously pleased with me, asked, "Well, son, now what?" at the breakfast table, and refrained from questioning me too closely about the tour. My mother waited for a week before telling me that she had suspected all along that my association with C. R. had ended abruptly.

It was at breakfast, just after my father again brought up the matter of my joining him in business, that I spoke with a conviction that surprised and impressed him. "No, Dad," I said, "I guess I won't be taking that job. I've decided that I'm going to be a newspaperman. I might even become a dramatic critic."

I realized, during the year following my return from Virginia, that the tour with Charles Richmond and the two months in Roanoke on my own had done a great deal for me. I had acquired self-confidence and a feeling of independence, and a desire to see a bit of the world. "Move about when you can, boy," Richmond often said. "Take some trips. See things and meet people. A man has to keep on broadening his horizons." My association with Richmond had given me, I also realized, tenacity and perseverance, and a determination to finish things that I started. C. R.'s solemn words, "You can get us an engagement in this town, boy, if you'll just try hard enough," had prepared me for the tactics of Managing Editor Sutlive, who always insisted that "there's no story a good reporter can't get."

Whatever became of my Shakespearean friend? I've indicated that he was a man of courtesy, wisdom, and tolerance, and that he gave scrupulous attention to the repayment of money he had borrowed. A year or so after I last saw him in Roanoke I received a letter postmarked Rutland, Vermont. There was a brief note, "Hope you now know who the Duke of Gloucester was, and that you've been reading up on my old friend, Polonius. Here's half of your original investment." He had enclosed a money order for $37.50.

Charles Richmond can never go out of my life. His influence upon me was educational and inspirational. I think of him often and I can still see him standing, lean and gaunt, and bag in hand, waiting his turn to board a dusty day coach. And I can still see him walking in the yellow sunshine of Bristol, Virginia–Tennessee, on a steaming summer day, umbrella under his arm, rehearsing the exalted speech of Prospero, or intoning—for his own enjoyment, and for mine— Antony's address to the Romans.

## chapter four

~~~~~~~~~~~~~~

GIGANTIC rats infested the editorial quarters of the *Savannah Press,* the city's afternoon daily. Bold as they were, incautious as they got to be by night, they remained within the crannied walls of the dingy old building during daylight hours. There was too much traffic for them, and Billy Sutlive's spasmodic roaring would have frightened them to death. But in the evening the city room became a rodents' playground. Those of the staff who occasionally went back to the office for work on overnight assignments had fears of actual attack as they sat nervously over their typewriters.

The *Press,* lively and newsy and outrageously helter-skelter in its make-up, occupied a crumbling three-story structure that stood on a Whitaker Street corner a block or so from the building of the *Morning News,* an older, sounder, stronger, and better-edited competitor. The business office of the *Press* used the ground floor, the editorial department had the second, and the top floor belonged to the composing room. It was a rickety stairway that led from street level to the editorial rooms.

I know, because my ascent of those stairs to ask for my first newspaper job remains one of the most terrifying of life's experiences. I faltered at the top step and considered a retreat. Then, quickly, in a now-or-never move and mood, I turned into the corridor, walked through a doorway, and was in the presence of the short, pudgy, flat-nosed Billy Sutlive, a south Georgia cyclone.

W. G. Sutlive, called Billy by thousands of Savannahians, had been in the employ of the *Press* ever since its establishment in 1891, moving from the circulation department into the editorial department. In 1915, with the paper's founder, Pleasant A. Stovall, abroad as Ambassador to Switzerland, Sutlive *was* the *Savannah Press*. He was its managing editor and was doubling as its editor. He knew just about everybody in the town. He was a mixer, a joiner, an organizer, a crusader, a raconteur, a lunchtime speaker, an after-dinner speaker, a street-corner listener, and greeter who could never walk half a block in downtown Savannah or go into any store without someone saying "Hi, Billy!" He knew the city, block by block; his contacts were endless, and the news tips that he received in a single day were often enough to keep his entire staff on the run. Ambassador Stovall, just before departing for Switzerland, remarked, "I don't have to worry about Willie getting the news. My only worry will be that he will get too much."

Sutlive, tireless, excitable, and able, never smoked. He drank only an occasional glass of sherry and only swore when he had to. He wore rimless spectacles and was always changing his glasses; he regarded bifocals as a plagued nuisance. He carried a pocket watch, an open-faced Waltham, wore suspenders, and liked riding on streetcars. He would never consent to be driven to work in the family automobile. Essentially a country boy, Sutlive found the streetcars folksy and cozy; there would generally be people to talk to, and it was his considerable influence that kept the city's last trolley line, the Habersham, in operation for some time after the power company had been ready to give it up for buses.

No editor in all the South had a desk that could outdo that of Billy Sutlive's in sheer untidiness, but he always insisted that he could, in a matter of seconds, put his hands on any desired clipping or letter buried in the great mass of litter rising threateningly on either side of his clanking Oliver. This stubby and incredibly energetic Jack-of-a-dozen-trades had one hobby and that was getting out a newspaper. His job in life, as he saw it, was to gather items to put in his paper, and he found a great deal that interested him—and his readers, he thought— in going through the country weeklies with care. Dozens of weeklies, down at the bottom of the pile, contributed to the daily disarray of his busy desk.

Billy Sutlive had a good mind, a savage wit, and a ready laugh. No man was quicker, upon occasion, to sarcasm, but no one could be gentler or more ingratiating. He was a man of humor, understanding, and a definite tolerance; he was also given to sudden bursts of anger, and when he got mad he was mad all over. A display of negligence or stupidity on the part of one of his reporters was likely to throw him into a rage. He was a great believer in the names-make-news theory of journalism and was fanatical on the subject of accuracy in spelling out names used in the *Press* stories. If the name of a pallbearer in the smallest obituary was spelled incorrectly it was generally Sutlive who would catch the error, in proof or in the first edition, and a roar would accompany such a discovery. "If a man serves as a pallbearer at a funeral, however obscure, it's important to him," he would say in his frequent talks to the staff, "and that man will be the very first to buy a copy of the paper to see if his name is in it. If we get the name wrong, or give him the wrong initial, we lose a subscriber." Sutlive was unable to understand how any staff member could ever misspell the name of a Savannahian who was listed in either the telephone book or the city directory, or both, and he often expressed the opinion that a good newspaperman was one who considered himself on duty at all times, twenty-four hours in every day. He once came upon two of his reporters sauntering together along Whitaker Street, an hour or so after the final edition had gone to press. He greeted them pleasantly but said he didn't like to find two staff members in the same street. "Next time," he said, "one of you take Whitaker and the other take Bull. We'll get more news that way."

All of the editorial hiring and firing at the *Press*, over a period of some years, was done by Billy Sutlive. He fixed the salaries and he gave the decisions on the requests for more money; such requests were infrequent and so were the increases. Sutlive, for all of the hours that he put in and for all of his value to the company—he kept the editorial costs down to an absolute minimum and he brought in untold thousands in advertising revenue by the mere fact of his presence—was himself grossly underpaid. But he lived comfortably, had a nice house in a pleasant residential section, and enough money to bring up a family.

A dollar went far in Savannah in 1915. Rent was cheap, so was clothing. Food cost little and a good meal was obtainable in a downtown restaurant for forty cents. The sum of $18 weekly was the average wage of an established, all-around reporter. The city editor of the all-powerful *Morning News* was getting only $22.50 in 1913 when he resigned to accept his appointment as the city's postmaster. Many a man went along, in those Savannah years from 1910 to 1917, supporting a wife and family on $25 a week. Staff members of the *Morning News* worked seven days weekly, with an occasional day off. They reported for assignments around noon and were on duty until midnight, sometimes until 2 A.M. A rugged schedule, but that was an era when newspapermen were in the game because of their sheer love of it, an era some years prior to the arrival of the demanding and high-flying Newspaper Guild, which was to bring banker's hours to the city room and the wages of an editor-in-chief to a reporter just graduated from the copy-boy status.

Billy Sutlive, in his own galvanic way, did the work of six men and expected as much from all members of his staff. He wrote the lead editorial every day, dashed off a humorous column, and clipped the Georgia papers, dailies and weeklies, that we called the "exchanges," with gigantic and venerable shears. He frequently pounded out news stories, did a great deal of the headline writing—the headline emphasis on many a local-page story was often unsupported by the story itself—

and he always served as make-up editor at press time. The *Press* printers, along with its reporters, liked him, respected him, and were somewhat terrified by him. They knew him to be a man of action, one to whom it was never too late to put a new lead on a news story. He would often crouch beside a Linotype machine and dictate his last-minute revisions to the operator.

Billy Sutlive gave considerable time to his favorite fraternal order, the Knights of Pythias. He could become fairly fanatical on the subject of the Civil War and the cause of the Confederacy, and he could tell you, in startlingly vivid detail, why the South should have won at Shiloh and why it did win at Chancellorsville. He found time for his churchgoing, which he took uncomplainingly, and for theatergoing, which he relished. Savannah was one of the busiest of the road towns prior to World War I; the touring companies came along in a season-long procession, and there was plenty of work for a dramatic critic. Sutlive was the *Press's* official reviewer and he covered all of the seemingly important productions. He had a hospitality for the theater as such and, never having more than a half hour for the writing of a notice and not wanting to ruin the business for a two-day attraction, he was frequently overfriendly. But when he got the notion that the city of Savannah and the state of Georgia were being imposed upon by Broadway managements in sending down shoddy scenery and fourth-rate actors, his review of the goings-on at the old Savannah could be epic in its scorn and severity. Many of the advance men knew Billy Sutlive well; they vastly enjoyed their calls at the *Press* office, and they were always entertained, as they sat beside his desk with mimeographed copy and pictures in hand, and waited for him to finish a red-hot editorial or to hammer out, upon his unprotesting Oliver, the last few quips of his "Bill Biffen" column, devoted to sage observations, anecdotal paragraphs, and odds and ends of Chatham County wit and wisdom.

When not antagonized by inferior companies playing the Savannah Theater (25 cents to $1.50 and, in the cases of engagements played by stars, 50 cents to $2), when not aroused by municipal thickheadedness or exasperated by the ineptness of his own staff, Billy Sutlive was a good-hearted and affable Georgian who loved his wife and children, paid his bills within reasonable time, and was forever thinking of the progress of his city, his county, and his state. He had a sense of fair dealing and an appreciation of friendship. He also had the capacity for fighting back when wronged and he could be ruthless in his retaliation. He once signed a bank note for one of his employees, a man then holding the post of city editor. That man, finding a job elsewhere, left Savannah abruptly, without giving the *Press* a day's notice and with only a few written words to Sutlive, bidding him a bleak good-by. Sutlive, greatly annoyed and deciding that he was stuck on that note, wrote a brief story, displayed in a prominent spot on the local page, setting forth that his ex-employee had skipped town, leaving many unpaid bills and old friends with the responsibility of settling his obligations.

Sutlive, a man with a positive passion for newspaper work, who enjoyed every minute in every hour that he was about the *Press* plant, was somehow of the impression that any man

70

lucky enough to be taken on his staff was more or less out of order in questioning the compensation allotted to him. Sutlive knew that his employees had little money but he got impatient with those who became involved financially. I don't know that he ever fired a man because of debts, but he would never fail to express himself with some vehemence. There was a time during my association with the *Press* when a telephone in the city room rang for some ten minutes just before going-to-press time, and it was left unanswered by two staff members who were present. A short time later Sutlive came tearing into the office. He was furious. "Where the hell has everybody been?" he shrieked. "Doesn't anybody ever stay around here any more? Don't you men know that *somebody* should always be here?"

"Why, we've been right here for the last hour, haven't we, Jim?" said a tall, easygoing Alabamian who had been on the staff two or three years. "Sure have," assented Jim. "Right here."

"All right," cried Sutlive, "why the hell didn't you answer the telephone?"

Both young men vowed that it hadn't rung.

"The hell it didn't ring," screamed Sutlive. "It rang because I was on the phone trying to tell my brilliant staff about a man jumping out of the window. But I couldn't get my brilliant staff to answer the goddam telephone because they were afraid that it was a creditor on the wire. Yes, a bill collector! And I defy either of you to look me in the eye and tell me what I'm saying isn't so."

Neither man looked him in the eye; neither man spoke.

Sutlive, having won his point, laughed. "Just what I thought," he said. "What kind of a newspaper are we trying to run?"

Then he ripped off coat and tie, shrieked "Boy!" for some copy paper, and sat down and wrote the story of the man jumping out of the window.

I got on the staff of the *Savannah Press* by the device of offering to work six months for no salary at all.

The *Press's* city editor, as of 1915, was William P. Flythe, a Georgian from Augusta—dark, lean, emaciated, and well liked in Savannah. He was a thoroughly experienced newspaperman, pounded a typewriter with two-fingered agility, and was frequently given to covering the city hall run. I'd seen him along Bull Street several times and once, as I was ushering at an evening performance at the Savannah Theater for the privilege of seeing John Drew and his company in Somerset Maugham's *Smith*, I'd shown City Editor Flythe to the wrong seat, thereby creating some confusion. When I decided that a newspaper job was my immediate objective I turned to the telephone book for Flythe's home address, a bit of a trick that all reporters should master early in their careers, and went out to his apartment in Lincoln Street around 8 P.M.

I timed the visit carefully so as to arrive when he was done with dinner. I wanted to find him when he was relaxing in his living room. I rang the bell and he came to the door. Very cordial, too. Sure, he knew about me; had always been wanting to see one of my amateur plays. Why didn't I come right in and sit down, and what was on my mind? For the next half hour I told him and he was all encouragement. Sure, that sounded like a good proposition, acquiring a great reporter at no cost to the paper. The *Press* was never, he observed, a paper that liked to hand out money recklessly and he was sure that the business office would approve of taking me on, and he thought I could be of some help to him. But. . . .

"You'll have to see Billy Sutlive," he said. "I can't do a thing without his okay. Nobody can. Tell you what you do. Show up around nine o'clock tomorrow morning. He'll be through his big editorial by then and he ought to be in a good humor. Show up there—and I wish you luck."

I showed up. I went into my speech as I had memorized it for an hour or so in strolling along Bay Street, the waterfront thoroughfare, and it was a sales talk delivered without a slip. He listened to me, nodded, and broke into a laugh.

"Hell," he said, "I thought you wanted to be an actor."

"I did," I said, "but no more. Perhaps sometimes a dramatic critic, but right now a reporter. . . . I'm ready to start this very minute."

Sutlive took me on. A tryout arrangement, no salary for six months, and then I'd be given $10 a week. Or I'd be "sent the hell back to the stage or to the railroad business—and in a hurry." Those were Sutlive's words, followed by his rasping laugh.

Well, in about three months, as I reported for work at 8 A.M., Bill Flythe said, "W. G. wants to see you."

"Anything the matter?" I asked quickly.

"Dunno," he said.

"Did I spell the name of another pallbearer wrong?"

Flythe glared at me. "Get on in there. W. G. doesn't like to be kept waiting."

I went "inside"—a partition that came within a foot of reaching the ceiling separated Sutlive's portion of the floor from the city room—and found him engaged in his shattering assault upon his old Oliver. He looked up and motioned me to a chair.

"I'm glad to tell you, young man," he said with great cordiality and humanity, "that we're putting you on the payroll. You'll get $9 per week. Not so much, but when I started I only got $5. I think you're going to make a newspaperman, but you've got to learn that we don't do things by telephone around here; we go out and see people. . . . Now get in there and get to work—and congratulations."

I wrote a sports-page column called "The Evening Dope" under the name of J. Alexander Finn during my first few months on the *Press* and did city-news odds and ends. In a city of considerably less than 100,000, as Savannah was in 1915, the pseudonym of Finn held no mystery for any of those *Press* readers inclined to be inquisitive about it, and one such reader was a fiery young man named Babe Vandervere or something like that. In writing a very special "Evening Dope" column I picked an all-Savannah scholastic football team, leaving out and leaving off Bubber Bryson, a swarthy and rugged high-school halfback. Bubber didn't protest, but his friend, the fellow named Babe, certainly did. He waited for me at a soda fountain one afternoon and beat me up. I told Sutlive about it and he roared. Then he said, "That's fine! You're getting some readers!"

I gave up writing for the sports page when I was assigned to the hotel run. Such an assignment brought me to the decision, at an early age, that anybody with the opportunity to enjoy the comforts and conveniences of hotel life is somewhat mad not to take it—and quick! For several years prior to beginning newspaper work I'd looked upon Savannah's magnificent Hotel DeSoto with awe and reverence. The DeSoto, opened in 1890, had great high ceilings and wide corridors, a structure of red brick and terra cotta that had brought forth laudatory comment from William Howard Taft when he was elaborately entertained beneath its roof in 1909. Famous road stars, playing the Savannah Theater, had stayed at the DeSoto; players of professional stock companies that came to our town had lived there, and there had been many a time when I'd seen the beautiful Irene Timmons, leading woman with the Schiller Players, studying her lines in a rocking chair at a far end of the broad veranda.

So, when I was at the top of the world as an authorized representative of the city's only afternoon paper and getting $9 per week for doing work that seemed easier than anything else possibly could be, I naturally took to the De Soto Hotel as my headquarters and second home. I sat on its veranda with the ease and authority of a paying guest, sat before its great open fire on chilly days, went frequently upon invitation into its elegant dining room, and visited in its luxurious suites during talks with the great and near-great who were always passing through.

75

Billie Burke, girlish and animated, red-headed and given to rippling laughter, fairly overwhelmed me; she was so devastating and delightful a personality I was hardly aware of the presence of an uncommunicative and seemingly diffident man named Ziegfeld who sat in on our interview and to whom, inexplicably enough, she appeared to be married. Will Rogers came along with his lariat and his homely ways without creating any great commotion; Clara Joel gave her beauty and her tears to the role of the heroine of *Within the Law*; Raymond Hitchcock contributed some droll observations to a hotel-veranda talk as he played the city in *The Beauty Shop*; Margaret Anglin, touring in *Lady Windermere's Fan*, rapturous in her appreciation of the beauty of Savannah, was fairly mystic in her talk of the importance of Greek tragedy to the theater, and City Editor Flythe became apoplectic when he tried to decipher my report of the conversation. Grantland Rice, assigned by the *New York Tribune* to cover the Savannah tryout of the new team of the New York Yankees, told me without batting an eye that he had been reading my stuff in the *Press* and thought it was great. And I have tried to believe ever since that Rice, a human and wise and generous man, was telling the truth in every syllable.

Maude Adams, the ever-elusive, inaccessible, and more or less invisible, came through in *The Legend of Leonora*, and by some sorcery got from her train to her hotel room without being seen by anybody at all. And she was later successful in getting out of the DeSoto and back to her drawing room without my getting anywhere near her, and notwithstanding the fact that I had accomplices posted at every exit. It's quite possible that she disappeared via the laundry. Anyway, when I returned to the *Press* office and reported no interview with Miss Adams I got an understanding nod from City Editor Flythe and something of a tirade from Billy Sutlive. That was his way. That was why the *Press* printed a lot of news. That was why working for him served to provide training that was to be useful throughout a lifetime. I never knew Sutlive to admit that any story was unobtainable; he just went along on the contention that a reporter who failed hadn't tried hard enough.

When the Leftwich Players came down from Broadway to take up a stock engagement at the hoodoo house, the Liberty Theater, they settled grandly enough beneath the DeSoto's hospitable roof. In pursuit of news and illustrious visitors, I came upon the gaunt and emphatic Alexander Leftwich, the company's director-producer, and wrote for that day's *Press* a piece about the company's arrival and its plans. Leftwich liked the story and offered me the job of press agent at the extraordinary wage of $25 weekly, nearly thrice what I was getting at the *Press*. I was on my way into the big money—I thought.

Well, the Leftwich Players, with such interesting but then obscure actors as Edward Arnold and Frank Morgan in leading roles, opened at the Liberty. They put on good plays, they did them well at a fifty-cent top price for evening performances, but Savannahians didn't respond. Leftwich and his co-workers ceased talking of the beauty of the South and the charm of Savannah. "Terrible place," muttered the character

77

man after the third profitless week. "The people here don't want the theater; just why Alex ever brought us down here I'll never know." Leftwich, glum and broke, announced during the fifth or sixth week that the company was closing. On the final night I went to him to collect my wages; I hadn't received a dime.

"Son," he said, "it's too bad. There's no money to give you. Get back to your little paper job and forget you ever saw me. Haven't you heard that we're stranded?"

I persisted. I was willing, under the circumstances, to settle for two weeks' pay. He didn't speak; he merely sat there in the Liberty box office, his long legs crossed, and glared at me through his thick-lens glasses.

Finally, he spoke. "I wonder," he said quietly, "if you will do me a favor. I wonder if you will get the hell out of my sight."

During my reportorial career with the *Press* I got in a lot of general work in addition to covering the hotel run, and also into a fair amount of trouble. A prominent society woman cabled the paper's owner, Pleasant A. Stovall, then in Switzerland, asking that I be fired for overestimating her jewel robbery loss by $100,000. I went all the way out to Thunderbolt at dawn one morning to fight a duel, with rifles, with another ardent young Savannahian, also attracted by a vivacious young woman of East Anderson Street, and had to be talked out of the whole idea by one Willard Garrard, who had come along as my second. I had retained my status as an unconquerable swain, but as a Lothario doomed to many defeats, as I moved from the classroom into the city room.

The helpful Mr. Garrard, as fidgety and as eloquent as he was talented, was a wild man on his own account. He had, by this time, distinguished himself as a member of the staff of the *Atlanta Journal*, the best newspaper in the state. He liked excitement and always did his utmost to create it when none existed. During the streetcar ride back into town from the marshy duelling ground beside the river at Thunderbolt—my antagonist and I had arrived at the scene with .22 rifles and three cartridges each—Garrard was as jumpy and as garrulous as he might have been had the duel been fought and won. He suggested that perhaps I was just too dramatic for a town no larger than Savannah.

"Hell," he said, "you ought to be getting into bigger time. You've been on the *Press* for about seven months. That's enough for you and for the paper, too—I would think. You had better get on up to Atlanta. Your Anderson Street girl is going to Agnes Scott College, isn't she? I'll get you a job on the *Atlanta Journal* and you'll be only six miles away from her. Then you can march right into Agnes Scott and kidnap her, or set fire to the college, or do anything you like. I'll talk to the *Journal's* city editor. He likes his reporters good and wild. You'll hear from me."

That was that, I thought. But a week later a letter from Garrard arrived. He had spoken with John Paschall, the city editor; he had told Paschall that the *Journal* should not go to press another time without me in its employ. I was told to come on at once—and at $17.50 weekly.

I went that evening to call on Billy Sutlive at his home. He sat with me on his porch. He talked humanly, quietly, understandingly. "Sure," he said, "there's a lot you can still learn at the *Press*, but it will be good for you to get out of your home town. I can give you a raise from $9 to $12 if you want to stay, but I think there'll be more opportunity for you upstate. If I were you I'd get on the Central of Georgia and go to Atlanta."

There were tears from my mother at breakfast the next morning when I gave the family the news. My father was quiet, but he did say that he thought it was a good idea. "Entirely on your own," he said. "Might be the making of you."

"I know what it means," sobbed my mother. "It means that you're gone, gone for good. . . . Oh, I knew this would happen and I just hate it, hate it."

She then wept uncontrollably. But she wasn't crying when she went with me to the dingy Central of Georgia station two nights later to put me aboard the nine o'clock train for Atlanta. She merely said, "We all love you. This is your home. Please come back often."

## chapter five

~~~~~~~~~~~~~~~

HARLLEE BRANCH was an unsparing tor-
mentor when he sat in on the city desk. A martinet, this
ex-printer, an extraordinarily resourceful news-getter on his
own account, and one who turned mediocre reporters into
good reporters by his unrelenting drive. He was brusque and
tactless—and got results. "Aleck," he said to me after I had
been with the *Atlanta Journal* only three days, "I think you
can become a better writer." So there was nothing to do but
become a better writer. He frequently enraged staff men with
the casual remark, "Now, you get the facts and I'll tell you
how to write it." He encouraged mass mutiny by passing
around one- and two-paragraph clippings from the morning
*Constitution*, inconsequential items that shouldn't have been
printed at all, with the word "Check," scribbled across them.
During my first week with the *Journal* I was successful in
bringing in a picture, snatched from a bureau, of a man who
had been killed in his own bed by a night prowler. Thereupon,
Branch decided that I was the paper's picture-stealing specialist. Thereafter, in the case of a murder or a suicide, I was

relieved of whatever I was doing and sent out in quest of art work. "Go in there and get that picture, Aleck," Branch would say. "You can get it if you really try." He didn't actually say, "Don't come back unless you do get it," but the effect was the same.

The "Aleck" came about on the very day that I reported for work in Forsyth Street, an hour or so after I had stepped off the train from Savannah.

"So your name's Ward, is it?" Branch said, weighing the matter, with the resolve to overrule my parents. "Well, we already have one Ward around here—that's Ward Greene, over there in the corner—and one is enough. Did you ever have any other name? Didn't anybody ever call you Mike or anything?"

I told him of my sports-writing nom de plume of J. Alexander Finn.

"Fine! From now on your name is Aleck. . . . Now, Aleck, let me see what in hell I can give you to do. We've decided that we should start you on police. . . ."

Harllee Branch, folksy and friendly in out-of-office moments, was so exacting and inquisitorial during his city-desk shifts—and later when he was promoted to the city editorship— that numerous members of the staff secretly despised him. There came a day when the make-up editor, nursing ill will for months, argued openly with him, grappled with him, and tried to push him out of a fourth-story window into Forsyth Street. Staff members muttered and growled about the H. B. dictatorship during all of the three and a half years that I worked for the *Journal*, but I never met the man who didn't concede that the tireless and peremptory Branch was a fellow of great ability. Everyone admitted that he ran a training school—and a damned good one.

He wasn't one to take any nonsense from his staff. There was a morning some months after I had gone to work for the *Journal* when I made a temperamental announcement to three fellow-reporters, Ward Greene, Donald Denny, and Isaac Shuman. We all shared quarters in the Chesterfield apartments. "I'm not going to work today," I said. "I'm tired of Camp Gordon. I don't feel like working; I'm taking the day off." And I asked that such a message be taken to Branch.

The boys said they'd find great pleasure in giving such news to the city editor; they believed that his reaction might enliven the morning in Forsyth Street.

My telephone rang within a half hour; Branch was on the wire.

"Aleck," he said, "are you sick?"

"No, I'm not sick."

"What's the matter?"

"Nothing, I'm just taking the day off. Not in the mood for work."

"I see," he said. "Well, that's a shame. We like you here at the *Journal*; you're proving yourself a valuable man. But you're not *that* valuable. . . . It's now five minutes past eight. If you don't call me within fifteen minutes and say you're on your way to cover Camp Gordon your connection with the *Atlanta Journal* has ended." Then he hung up.

Fourteen and a half minutes later I called him. I went to Camp Gordon.

83

Branch was a devoted family man. He loved his wife and he was proud of his bright children. He wanted them to have all the educational advantages that had been denied to him and he went along on the understandable theory of the good American provider—that the harder he worked the more he was helping his family; and in all fairness, it should be recorded that he didn't drive his reporters in any sense of self-gratification or self-glorification. He merely felt that it was a part of his job.

Branch got his results with tactics directly opposed to those of John Paschall, the regular city editor at the time of my arrival, who later became managing editor and executive editor. Paschall was a wise, patient, and understanding executive. He had been with the paper since he came out of Vanderbilt University, just after the turn of the century. When Paschall said, in that ingratiating drawl that he had, "Aleck, I don't want you to set fire to the house or kill the widow but maybe you can go out and get a picture of a fellow who has just shot himself after throwing their three kids out of the window," I knew that I was sure to return with the picture. And when he pulled up a chair alongside my desk one day and said, "Aleck, I don't want you to get the paper into any trouble or yourself into any either, but it might make a hell of a story if you could sort of slip into that German prison camp out at Fort McPherson and tell us what it's like," I was already making my plans. The next day a major in the medical corps took me through and my resulting story was a one-day sensation.

There were some brilliant men in the Atlanta newspaper

field from 1916 to 1919. Britt Craig was a reporter of the gladiatorial school—swashbuckling, ruffianly, and irresistible. Anything for a story and more than anything, including honor, for a news beat. Tall, lithe, good-looking, pugnacious, he was the star of the *Constitution's* staff and one of the few men of that paper that the *Journal's* city room respected. Craig wasn't one to accept reportorial defeat in gentlemanly fashion. If he scored the beat he was amiable enough; when a *Journal* or a *Georgian* reporter came through with what he didn't have he got mad. I was with him on an assignment with troops in the Great Smokies of North Carolina and telephoned in a story that was elaborately displayed on page one. The *Constitution* told him about it and he came tearing into my hotel room in the town of Murphy, North Carolina. "Listen, you four-eyed little bastard," he roared, "people don't do that to Britt Craig. If that ever happens again I'll kick hell out of you."

Angus Perkerson, editor of the Sunday magazine, was fretful and meticulous. He did a story so thoroughly, so professionally, so brilliantly, he was frequently drafted by the city desk to handle important killings, of which there were many. And I fell in line with the enthusiasm of the entire plant, from publisher to copy boys, for Ward Greene's facility at the typewriter. "Read that boy's stuff," commanded Branch on the second day of my employment. "Read it—and try to get that good. When Jimmy Greene writes it's like butter on battercakes."

Laurence Stallings was an egotistical, garrulous, boyish, and well-read $12-a-week reporter who had been graduated from Wake Forest College and was out to make himself a fortune. Linton K. Starr was an interesting Atlantian—a fixer, a mixer,

85

one of the most engaging promoters of his time. He was the original man who could get it for you wholesale. He was the paper's state news editor when I first met him, but he had countless side lines—and many mystifying ways. In later years, some four or five after I had left Atlanta for New York, I returned to Georgia on a vacation and was taken by Starr to the north Georgia mountains for a week-end party. There were four of us as his guests, and he put us up in the crude lodge to which Margaret Mitchell and John Marsh had gone for their honeymoon. There was a great deal of rowdyism and corn-liquor drinking. The bride and groom dreaded the invasion and were ready to quit the mountain country, but a violent storm came up and there was no escape. Finally, along about midnight, Starr reached a decision and made a singular ruling. "We've disturbed the young couple enough," he said. "Rain or no rain, we're getting the hell out of here. There's another place, about a mile down the road. We'll get soaked, and probably struck by lightning, but we're going there." And we did.

Margaret Mitchell had not then written *Gone With the Wind* but she had done fine work as a member of the *Journal* staff, whose members always included a swarm of potential short-story writers, novelists, and playwrights. The glory of Joel Chandler Harris had never dimmed for Georgians and Atlantians; Corra Harris's success in fiction had a stimulating effect upon many a young reporter in the state, and the ease with which Jacques Futrelle, a *Journal* staff man, had turned to novel-writing left a definite impression in the city room.

I recall the stir created when Ward Greene sold his first story, *Peach Blossoms*, to *All-Story* magazine, for twenty-five dollars and the considerably greater hullabaloo that was brought about a few weeks later when the same magazine accepted my own *Thunder City's Great Idea* for forty dollars. "My God," remarked John Paschall, "what are we coming to and how are we going to get out a newspaper? We've got nothing around here except authors."

And there was the advent of a young reporter named Harold Ross, skinny and odd-looking, who made an impact of his own upon the Atlanta scene. He came along in 1913 and he vanished after a short time; there was still lively and seemingly endless city-room talk of him when I arrived three years later.

Ross, who was later to gain renown through his connection with the overseas daily, the *Stars and Stripes*, during World War I, and whose editorship of the *New Yorker* won for him the respect of the writing craft of a nation, was a restless boy-reporter in New Orleans prior to going to Georgia. He was a stray, a drifter in the fashion of the day; not rooted at all, and looking around. But he liked New Orleans in the winter, as did many newsmen of a migratory turn of mind; there was no need of buying an overcoat. It was at this time that Hearst, having acquired the *Atlanta Georgian*, was trying to revitalize it with metropolitan newspaper tactics, and by sending down high-powered reporters from New York and Chicago. There was also the feeling that some Southern talent was necessary in the setup and Ross was offered a job by a representative in New Orleans who appeared to have authority.

Ross wasn't one to ask for a guarantee or to give one; he just quit the *Item* and went to Atlanta. He found himself jobless in the Peachtree Street area when the *Georgian* and Mike Clofine, its sharp and decisive city editor, repudiated the fellow who had done that hiring in New Orleans. Ross went around to the *Journal*, met the shrewd and able and friendly John Paschall, and talked himself into a job.

Now this was not long after Atlanta, a state capital in which things are always happening, had witnessed the spectacle of Police Chief Beavers' vice squad descending upon the houses of the doomed red-light district with axes, a procedure that was legal under an old statute, and just before the tumult of the sensational Leo Frank case began.

Anyway, the alert and gawky-looking Ross, a newcomer with a capacity of his own for eruption and excitement, was assigned to the police run and found himself battling with some of Hearst's highly paid specialists ($35-a-week boys, phenomenal for Atlanta at the time) and befriended by the *Atlanta Constitution*'s Britt Craig, who resented the invasion of imported talent. He took Ross to an attic hideaway, which provided a ceiling peephole and eavesdropping privileges directly above the desk of the chief of police. Notwithstanding this advantage, Ross took a considerable pushing around from Hearst's big-city operators and there came the day when he was sent to the Fulton Tower to see a man brought back from Mexico on charges of embezzlement; he'd crossed the border with a vast supply of currency and had also taken along a girl.

88

An important story and a good one; there was everything against the fellow except charges of horse stealing and arson. But the prisoner was not to be seen. Not even for a minute.

Ross then learned that the man had refused himself to the *Journal* and the *Constitution* because he had sold out to the *Georgian* which, in accordance with a Hearst practice of the time, had paid him $500 for the exclusive rights to his story. The *Georgian* had taken his pictures in the jail and had decided to run the story in a series of articles, over the course of a week. Ross was fairly desperate until he got to talking to an Atlantian who was hanging about the *Journal* office—a member of the Masonic order, who had remarked that the embezzler was also a Mason. "Well," suggested Ross quickly, "shouldn't you Masons do something about helping out the poor bastard?" Certainly should, the man agreed, and within a short time he was at the man's cell, with Ross at his side, giving a sympathetic ear to the prisoner's detailed, two-hour story of absconding to Mexico.

Ross raced to Harllee Branch with his news. Branch called John Paschall and then Jack Cohen was reached; there was great elation. Here was the *Journal's* chance to give the *Georgian* and its gentleman-gangsters the kind of beating it deserved and would understand. "We'll break the story tomorrow," decided Paschall. "Wouldn't it be great if we had a picture of the fellow to go with it?" Well, there was then nothing for Harold Ross to do but say that he would get a picture. He waited until late afternoon, until he knew that the *Georgian's* Alabama Street plant would be just about deserted, and then he entered the building from the rear, via the railroad tracks that cleaved the city. He found his way to the staff photographer's darkroom, came upon a great array of plates, many of them of the man in the Tower, picked out two good ones, and went back to the *Journal* office. He was at his typewriter for most of the night; his story carried his by-line and it appeared in all editions.

The *Georgian* became suddenly holy, charging burglary in a formal protest to the *Journal's* president, and quite forgetting for the moment that its own tactics had included the use of dynamite, if necessary, to get a desired photograph.

Harold Ross was established as a hero in Forsyth Street; he was told that he had found his home. But the Colorado-born boy-reporter had begun to get itchy feet; for some time he had been longing to get to the North and had developed a loathing for Atlanta's dead, dull, shut-up-tight Sundays. For some weeks he'd told himself that he just wouldn't spend another Sunday in Atlanta. And on a Saturday he left, as unceremoniously as he had arrived. In a note he tried to say it was some sort of family illness. But John Paschall well knew that a good and restless reporter had just decided that it was time to move on.

There was no great difficulty for a young man of eighteen, with no one to look out for but himself, to live well on $17.50 weekly in a Southern city in 1916. I paid $2.50 per week for a room at the Y, ate all my meals in cafeterias, greatly enjoyed the experience of being away from my home town, and this time I well knew that I would never return except for visits.

I was on my own, whatever the outcome was to be. Sometime after my arrival in Atlanta I was invited by the friendly Estes Doremus to share his large room in the fashionable Pickwick apartments and I was unable to resist this new luxury. I realized, all over again, that my fondness for staying around the beautiful Hotel DeSoto in Savannah had given me a yearning for a way of life, that I was permanently and irrevocably hotel-struck. In fact within another year or so I found myself making a deal with the Georgian-Terrace, the city's finest hotel, to take up quarters there at the extraordinarily reasonable press rate of ten dollars weekly, exactly half of what the *Journal* was paying me. But by then I had begun taking on "outside work" as we called it, doing publicity for two or three of the local film houses. The best of these jobs was that of exploiting the glories of the film house that showed Universal Pictures exclusively. I always thought they were pretty dreadful, but in hiring me the exhibitor was particularly insistent on one point —I would have to *see* all movies before writing about them. It was frequently toturesome.

For my first six months in Atlanta I covered police. The seeing of dead and mangled people—suicides, victims of shooting and cutting scrapes and automobile accidents—became a daily experience. I got to know and to like the cops—simple, friendly, unschooled, underpaid, and generally decent people. I rode with them on emergency calls in their Model Ts, talked with them during long and quiet hours at the Decatur Street headquarters, visited them at their homes, and eventually put on, with a cast of Atlanta amateurs, a performance of Paul Armstrong's melodrama, *Alias Jimmy Valentine*, which brought twelve hundred dollars into the funds of the police relief association. I was slimmer, stronger, and sounder, if no taller, in that day and took over the role of the sentimental and romantic Valentine, who risks breaking his alibi and going back to prison by returning to safecracking in an emergency, such being the saving of the life of the heroine's little sister, who has been accidentally locked in the big vault. We did the play for one triumphant performance at the premier Georgia playhouse, the Atlanta Theater, and then for another performance at the federal penitentiary, and before the most responsive audience I've ever known. The convicts roared when Valentine scored a point over the dogged Detective Doyle; they cheered him in his love scenes with the banker's beautiful daughter. I had done all the casting for our production and during rehearsals fell utterly in love (the fifth or sixth time by now) with the leading lady, a slim, dark-haired, fiery, seventeen-year-old Atlanta girl named Elvena Neal. She received roses on the opening night from the *Journal's* real-estate editor. Three months later she eloped with him. It was her decision that he represented stability.

A fellow actor in that cast of *Alias Jimmy Valentine*, James A. Belflower, was police reporter on the *Journal's* afternoon competitor, Hearst's lively and always-in-the-red *Atlanta Georgian*. He was a remarkably industrious fellow—a digger, a plugger, a tireless reporter, and he gave me no end of friendly counsel during my first month or so on the police run. Once he decided that I could take care of myself, he began trying to scoop hell out of me, and I took to the warfare with relish. Bell and I were good friends in off hours, deadly enemies from

92

7:30 A.M. to 3. Belflower supported a family on a meager reportorial wage and later increased his income by taking up the
practice of law, valiantly defending many of those tried in the
court he was covering for the *Georgian.*

In those police-reporting days I got to know thugs, counter-
feiters, dope fiends, and prostitutes. The city's elaborate and
police-regulated red-light district had been abolished before
my time in Atlanta, closed during the regime of that conscientious and fine-looking cop, Chief Beavers, and the whores were
now scattered all over town. One of the prettiest creatures I
ever set eyes upon was a girl of sixteen arrested on charges of
conduct unbecoming a minor; she admitted to Recorder
George E. Johnson, an erstwhile candy manufacturer, a jocose
fellow who might have come right out of Gilbert & Sullivan,
that she had had intimacy with twenty-two men in a single
night and had earned more than one hundred dollars. When
I saw her in the detention rooms of the women prisoners at
police headquarters she made a proposition—she'd spend the
night with me, when the opportunity came around, if I'd put
in a long-distance call for her and give a message to a friend
in Selma, Alabama. It was a Mr. H. and I was to tell him that
she was ill and needed two hundred dollars; he had been her
great friend and she knew he wouldn't fail her; he must never
know the truth of her immediate plight. She hadn't finished
with all the hurried details for my emergency call when the
matron announced a visitor—a tall, graying, dignified gentleman had come to her rescue. Two hours later, after working
out an arrangement with the humane Recorder Johnson, the
beautiful little trollop went back to Selma with Mr. H.

Taxi drivers and bellboys in the Atlanta of 1916–1917 had their lists of call girls, and there were numerous hotels in which prostitutes lived and practiced their trade without molestation from the management, and often by sharing profits with bellmen, doormen, and even desk clerks. It became known to some of us at the *Journal* that a sedate and apparently sinless staff member, a bachelor who had always appeared to be something of a misogamist, disappeared from the office for an hour or so every few weeks and took himself, with all precautionary devices, to a hotel that knew him, liked him, understood him, and rented him a room on a day rate without ever a word of comment or a glance. The bellmen then supplied the girls.

I went along with general assignments after being taken off police, reporting at the office at 7:30 A.M and generally being off by 4, and in the afternoons and evenings did a great deal of moviegoing and theatergoing. The silent pictures of that time were the films of Essanay and Vitagraph, Pathe and Kalem, Biograph and Lubin and Paramount-Famous Players; the stars of that voiceless era included such legendary folk as Marguerite Clark and Mary Pickford, William S. Hart and Max Linder, King Baggot and Dustin Farnum, Bushman & Bayne and Clara Kimball Young and Norma Talmadge and Lillian Walker. Big-time vaudeville asserted itself at the Forsyth—Alan Dinehart had one of the most engaging variety sketches ever written in *The Meanest Man in the World*— and the old Atlanta Theater provided a stage for the on-from-Broadway companies sent down into the South. I had a whirl at dramatic criticism for some months—and that meant getting to the office well before the regular time in the morning to have the play review written before the city desk swung into action—and for nearly half a year—got out the Sunday magazine. It was a great moment, at the age of nineteen, when John Paschall called me over to the city desk and said, "Aleck, Mr. Perkerson is sick. He may be out for a long time. Get in there and run the magazine. That's your job until Perk returns." I came to realize during the next few months how thorough, how imaginative, and how news-wise Angus Perkerson really was.

During my Atlanta play reviewing I gave my most rapturous notice to the D. W. Griffith film *The Birth of a Nation* on tour as a regular road attraction and at a $2 top, and my worst to *Peg O' My Heart*, which had been coming along for several seasons. The company seemed to be awful, and so I reported, having kind words only for the dog in the cast. Two days later the entire troupe called at the *Journal* office to protest to the editor—and to take me by the throat if I happened to be around. It was my good luck that I'd been sent out to Stone Mountain. Some years later I met one of those *Peg* players at the bar of The Lambs club in New York. "Morehouse? Morehead? Morehouse?" this actor repeated. "Fellow by that name gave us such a lousy notice down in Georgia we had to close the tour. That couldn't have been you, could it?" "Me?" I said, in all innocence. "I was never in the state of Georgia in all my life."

When America entered the war in 1917 I was assigned to cover Camp Gordon, a training cantonment of enormous acreage. Harllee Branch said to me, "Aleck, it's an awful big place and I could probably get the *Journal* to buy you a motor-cycle, but you'd kill yourself and we don't want to lose you as a reporter. So you'd better do the job on foot."

I did the job on foot and tried to make friends with the military as I had with the cops. I was successful in getting at least a dozen big exclusive stories, to the great chagrin of the *Georgian* and the *Constitution*, and I'm sure that my greatest news source was the profane, realistic, friendly Colonel Preston Brown, a man of ferocious visage, who served as chief of staff for the 82d Division. Colonel Brown, snarling one instant and smiling the next, would glare at me with the remark, "You here again? You've become a goddam nuisance. Now get the hell out of my sight." Five minutes later, as I waited outside, I'd be told that the Colonel wanted me. Then, as if seeing me for the first time, he would say, "Where've you been? Why don't you hang around? Get out your pencil. Here's a story that will let you beat the Christ out of the *Constitution*."

By 1918 I was living in the beautiful Georgian-Terrace, taking dancing lessons from its instructor, a suave, slim, and mysterious young man named Arthur Murray, and occasionally I got a welcome break from the office routine by being sent on trips into the Blue Ridge Mountains to bring back corn liquor in great jugs for *Journal* executives. I was a safe man for such assignments; I'd never had a drink in all my nineteen years.

I vastly enjoyed living at the Georgian-Terrace, notwithstanding the fact that I was ever subject to the I-wonder-if-that-young-man-belongs-here scrutiny from wealthy dowagers who rocked on the broad Peachtree Street terrace. And I thought I was making fair progress under the tutelage of Professor Murray (he was then talking dreamily of making a million by teaching dancing by mail), but got into a bit of trouble at a hotel supper dance. The music called for a fox trot. My partner was an elegant matron belonging to the top brackets of Atlanta society and I got confused, going gaily into a one-step. Mrs. D. struggled to keep up with me. "My!" she cried, "you *are* in a bit of a hurry."

We got back to our table and sat the next one out.

Working for such taskmasters as Billy Sutlive of Savannah and Harllee Branch of Atlanta prepared reporters for a great variety of experiences. Branch, besides impressing me with the fact that a good man didn't return to the office with a report of nonsuccess on an assignment, also provided, for his entire staff, training for coolness under threat of gunfire. There was a doctor in Atlanta, mildly demented, who was of the notion that he had been done a wrong by Branch and resolved to kill him. He made a more or less general announcement of such intention, gabbling idly about it to uneasy patients, and he came one morning into the office of the advertising manager of the *Journal*, thrust a gun against his belly, and said, "This is how Branch is going to get it—where is he?" On another day—and this was a day during which Branch was absent from the office—Doc got on the elevator, rode to the fourth-floor city room, sauntered up to the city desk, and with his right hand in his pocket, asked menacingly enough, "Where's Harllee?"

Branch went to his attorney. He put his problem before

97

this hard-headed, Georgia-born lawyer, who listened in deep silence. Then he made his decision: "This crazy man is trying to take your life. If you feel that it's worth saving you've got to defend yourself. You can't expect anybody to do it for you. You've got to get a gun, learn to shoot it, and shoot it straight. The idea is, Harllee, that you must kill the old doctor before he kills you."

Well, Branch got himself a gun. He took target practice, going out into the woods daily and shooting at the trees. He got so that he could hit a tree—even a thin one—and he became convinced that he was enough of a marksman to stop the Doc, in a charge across the city room, without killing any of his reporters. For weeks all of this went on and for weeks there was tension at the *Journal* plant. I was one of the supposedly quick-of-foot staff members and was given the desk nearest the door that opened on the corridor, and it was my assignment to call out a warning if I saw the Doc coming through. Just behind me sat Rogers Winter, with a revolver in his top drawer, and on beyond Winter there was Branch on the city editor's platform, his gun beneath sheets of copy paper, and always within six inches of his right hand.

The day came when Branch, arriving for work at 7:30 A.M., found the bloodthirsty Doc, pale and unshaven, waiting for him on the narrow viaduct walk that ran alongside the *Journal* building, above the railroad tracks. This was the test and he knew that he had to meet it. He moved toward the Doc without a faltering step and when he was within ten feet of the now indecisive gunman he said: "Doc, if you make one move it will be your last one."

The Doc reacted strangely. He half raised his arm, assumed an air of jocularity and something of a how-are-you-Harllee-old-boy attitude, and extended a weaponless hand. Branch, having won the Battle of the Viaduct, was in no mood for handshaking. He merely said, "Go on home and quit making a fool of yourself." He then stepped past the Doc and walked briskly into the building.

There was no more copy reading from our city editor with a revolver at his elbow.

During those Atlanta years I was beaten up two or three times and, on two occasions, at least, needed a bit of luck to escape death. On the first airplane ride of my life—the year was 1918—I climbed into a two-seated, single-motored plane with an army lieutenant, a man of scant flying experience, who had been stationed in the Atlanta area for a short time. He set out for La Grange, Georgia, with plenty of daylight necessary for the short trip, but he was unfamiliar with the terrain, he didn't read his map correctly, and darkness came on by the time we reached our destination. My pilot, shrieking down for directions to the flying field, circled at 200 feet above the town's business section. Finally, directed by the frantic arm waving of people in the streets, he zoomed off in the direction that he decided was the right one, and found the baseball park. That looked good enough for Lieutenant Wilson. He throttled down, swung in low, barely missing the grandstand, and spun to a crash landing ten feet from home plate. His plane was cracked up; we both came out of it with a few bruises.

Then there was the week end when I was on an expedition out in the north Georgia mountain country with troops from Camp Gordon. Something of a man hunt, as I recall it. I rode for a great deal of the time in a huge army truck with the detachment of infantrymen and some of the time with the officers in a small car. The officers' car, leading the truck, came to a sudden stop about one hundred feet from a river. The commander of the expedition sprang from the car and began looking at a map. I scuttled down from the truck to see what the delay was all about, such being the privilege and the duty of the press. It seemed that Major J. had thought that we had come along the wrong road and it was then decided that we weren't lost—that there was a turn to be made *after* we crossed the river via a huge covered bridge, ancient and wooden. The officers looked at the bridge but no one said, "That damn thing doesn't look safe." It later seemed odd that, during the five-minute pause, not a man expressed the thought that perhaps an obviously antiquated structure, used for years by back-country vehicles, many of them horse-drawn, might not be strong enough to bear the weight of a gigantic army truck loaded with thirty soldiers, all carrying arms.

I had started back to the truck to join the troops when the lieutenant who was driving the advance car called to me. I turned, went to him, and got in with the officers. The procession began moving again. We rattled on across, getting glimpses of sluggish yellow water, twenty to thirty feet below, through chinks in the planking. We had moved along about fifty yards on the other side of the river when there came a violent crash from the enclosed bridge. "God," said the major, his face white, "what was that?"

The lieutenant stopped the car, I raced back to the bridge entrance and saw a great rent in the structure, just about midway. The big truck had dropped into the water. A dozen men, including a young and eager Brooklyn corporal with whom I'd been talking five minutes before, died in that accident. A dozen others were severely injured. I can still hear the moans of a sergeant, blinded, crushed, and in terrible pain, pleading for someone to put a bullet through his head.

Perhaps I wasn't the world's best reporter when I left Atlanta for New York late in the fall of 1919, but I was proud of my reportorial achievements and it had been a period of more or less continuous excitement. There was always something on: troops, golf champions, football championships, the frenzy of politics, vice raids, the Metropolitan Opera, building booms, fires, murders, and suicides. It's possible that the trend toward homicide was no greater in Atlanta than in other swiftly growing cities of its size and importance, but the *Journal's* make-up editor always seemed to be holding space on page one for an interesting and impromptu local killing. Atlanta suicides appeared to be a bit more dramatic than they were elsewhere. I came to believe, out of personal experience, that in walking about the city's streets everybody should always be looking up, as well as to the right and to the left. In crossing Five Points at an early hour one morning, en route to the office, a man who had jumped from the fifteenth story of a bank building missed me by ten feet. I was smeared by brains and blood, which splashed over the Marietta Street sidewalk from curb to building line.

Interesting people came to Atlanta: war heroes, painters, explorers, editors, stars of the stage, stars of the Met. I was once given the assignment of living in Caruso's suite for two days and following him about; I was told to be host to Jeanne Eagels, coming through in a play prior to her fame in *Rain*, by giving her a genuine home-cooked Southern meal and putting it all on an expense account. When Arthur Brisbane and Frank A. Munsey called upon Editor Jack Cohen and expressed the desire to be taken through the Atlanta penitentiary I was relieved of an irksome city-room task and given the tour-conducting job for the day. Brisbane talked almost continuously and always entertainingly; Munsey was silent for most of the time. And there was, again, futile pursuit of Maude Adams, this time when she reached Atlanta in Barrie's *A Kiss for Cinderella*. (For the record let it be set forth that I finally caught up with Miss Adams in New York in 1932, being her luncheon guest at the Colony Club. Two hours of enchantment.)

Yes, Atlanta was a hell of a newsy town. I had a good job and seemed certain of keeping it, I had many friends in town and was a Georgian with a lively appreciation of his home state. So what was all the nonsense about wanting to break away from a setup of comfort and security and take up life in a strange environment?

Well, there was that urge not uncommon to thousands of

young reporters throughout the years to get to New York, to work in New York, to cover assignments in New York. But didn't I know that sitting through a banquet in the North and reporting on the speeches could be just as tedious as it was in Georgia? Yes, but there were bigger stories in New York. Sensational stories. Harry Thaw's killing of Stanford White. The Rosenthal-Becker case. The return of the survivors of the *Titanic*—and of the *Lusitania*. The return of Alvin York. The actors' strike. Well, what of it? Hadn't Atlanta had the Leo Frank case, the Daisy Grace case, and the golfing triumphs of Bobby Jones? Wasn't it the news center and the great crossroads city of the entire South? And didn't I realize that working in New York might mean a complete sacrifice of individuality and initiative? Reporters up there worked in packs; they divided their news. I might not like that.

I was talking it all over with the impeccable Estes Doremus, who was of a Georgia-for-the-Georgians turn of mind. Why the hell was I leaving, really? Did I want a raise? That could probably be arranged. A request for an increase from my current wage of $32.50 to $35 might be in order if the office knew that the additional $2.50 would keep me in town. Did I want a larger room at the Georgian-Terrace? One facing Peachtree Street or Ponce de Leon Avenue? That, also, could be arranged. Did I want to take Geraldine Farrar out the next time she came to Atlanta? Major Cohen could fix that. He knew her well.

"Just what the hell is it, Aleck?" asked Doremus, as he pounded the table during our midnight talk in the Room of the Blinking Owls at Atlanta's Hotel Ansley. "What is it you want? Do you want to have Jimmy Greene kicked off the paper so that you can get his good new typewriter? Do you want to have your desk moved down into the society department next to Isabelle Thomas? What do you want? It can be done. Tell Papa."

"The truth is," I said weakly, "I just want to go to New York, to be in New York, to live in New York, to work in New York."

"What the hell has New York got that we haven't got right here?"

"I'll tell you," I said quickly. "It has the theater. It has theaters. It has plays, running all the time, dozens of plays. Thousands of actors. I'll be within a subway ride of thirty, forty, fifty theaters. I'll be on Broadway!"

I realized my error as I spoke. Estes Doremus didn't speak; just looked at me. He took a gulp of his Coca-Cola. Kept staring for a minute or so. Then he said quietly, "Why didn't you tell me that in the first place? It all now makes sense. I now understand. You're still stage-crazy. I think you should walk into the office tomorrow morning, go right up to Harllee Branch and say, 'Harllee, I'm leaving the *Journal*; I'm going to New York.'"

I did.

## chapter six

~~~~~~~~~~~~~~~

DURING my first winter in New York, beginning in November of 1919, I found myself greatly impressed by the quality of the news writing in the city's daily press. There was often magic in the phrasing in stories without by-lines that appeared in the morning *World* and the *Tribune*. It also became apparent to one accustomed to overwork on a Southern daily that reporters in the North took it a bit easier and that many of the stars in the New York field were definitely personalities.

I never even saw the reputedly colorful managing editor with whom I had had correspondence about joining the staff of the *New York Tribune*—he had vanished, after some disagreement with the management, a day or so before I put in an appearance at 154 Nassau Street—but he could hardly have been more picturesque than some of my co-workers in the city room and competitors in the coverage of day-to-day assignments. These were men and women from all over—from New York City itself, from the Middle West, and the Southwest, from the Carolinas and the Dakotas, from New England

and the Pacific coast. Many of them had come on to New York as I had—eagerly, tremulously, wonderingly, but resolutely—and were being toughened by the transition that turns a midlander into a New Yorker.

The *New York Tribune*, at the time I rushed in upon the metropolis without bringing on any perceptible earth tremors, was undoubtedly a losing proposition on the business side, but it had an extraordinarily able editorial staff, and any new and supposedly bright boy, fortunate enough to get employment in the city room, was more or less awed by some of the staff's outstanding members.

Boyden Sparkes was a big, aggressive, and resourceful reporter, a man with a feeling for intricate and elusive detail in a story, with a sense of the theatrical—and he could write like hell. Always on the offensive and never entirely accepting the trustworthiness of his fellow man, Sparkes wasn't likely to be outwitted by any individual or any organization trying to victimize or humbug his paper. Sparkes didn't get the assignment on the T. R. Zann story, that of the gentleman from Zanesville, Ohio, who registered at the Hotel Belleclaire and called down to the desk for five pounds of raw meat for the lion he had in his room, all of it a build-up for the forthcoming film, *Tarzan*. But he did do the *Tribune's* reporting and writing in connection with the uproar created by the supposed abduction of a beautiful Turkish maiden from her native land. Eight Turks had been rounded up in the tangled thoroughfares in the vicinity of New York's Chatham Square, given baths and titles, along with gold-incrusted turbans and lavish Near Eastern attire, and been carefully instructed for two weeks. They were to represent members of a Turkish mission, come to New York to search for the beautiful Sari, a daughter of royal blood, and said to be held prisoner by her abductor in some corner of the great city. The most intelligent of the bewildered Turks was appointed sheik. Finally, the solemn gentlemen from the world of the mosques and the minarets were exposed to the scrutiny of the eager New York press. Columns and columns were written of them and their quest; their raiment was described in great detail. It all made good reading. The relentless Sparkes did his own share of descriptive writing, but, being as sharp-eyed as he was quarrelsome, he became suspicious when he noticed that the starched cuffs of the delegation barely visible beneath the elaborate outer garments, had the look of the collar-and-cuff industry of upstate New York. Of Troy, New York, maybe. The aroused Sparkes got Henry Morgenthau, Sr., on the telephone, and Mr. Morgenthau, who had just returned from diplomatic service in Turkey, told him, ever so quietly, that Sheik Ben Mohamed was a fake and a blasted liar. Sparkes then exposed the hoax of the Universal film company, which was just about to release a costly picture, *The Virgin of Stamboul*.

M. Jay Racusin, excitable and irrepressible, a thorough and conscientious reporter, was the *Tribune's* specialist in crime at the time I arrived, but there were still legends of his own debut. To get him out of the way on his first day at work, he was told to go and interview J. P. Morgan. He did so, returned to the office, and wrote the story. But it wasn't accepted or believed; the copy was never sent to the composing room. The news-service man, however, got a carbon of Rac's story, decided that it was something very special, and peddled it to the papers in all parts of the country. The early editions of the *World* and the *Herald* came in with the Morgan interview on page one. Chicago had sold the story back to the *Tribune's* opposition!

I was awed, and undoubtedly fascinated, by other members of the *Tribune's* editorial personnel in 1920. Lester Markel, slim and dark and scowling, the brilliant assistant managing editor, whose sardonic strain seemed something of a cover-up for his own innate shyness, sent me up to Columbia University to interview Professor Jacoby on the Einstein Theory. The professor talked, keeping it all as unscientific as possible, and we went along some twenty minutes. Suddenly, he paused and said, "I want to get paid for this. How much?" I telephoned Markel and told him that I was getting the interview but that the professor wanted money. "Good God!" said Markel. "I didn't know there was a businessman on Morningside Heights. . . . Tell him we'll give him fifty dollars." I did so. Professor Jacoby nodded, I picked up my pencil and copy paper, and the interview was resumed.

Frederick Beecher Edwards, a pale and slender newsman, a Canadian who could turn out a feature story with the touch of a master, seemed impressed when I showed him a check I'd received from *Munsey's Magazine* for a piece of fiction. "Well," he said, "how long has this been going on? I think I'll try it." In his spare time on the late rewrite trick in half a week he turned out a long short story, sent it to the *Saturday Evening Post,* and became something of the office idol a week later when he received a check for four hundred dollars, a

sizable sum in the market of that time. And then there was
Arthur James Pegler. He was a man of such color and such
violence and vehemence I thought he ought to be put into a
play. Much of the snarling from the leading character in my
newspaper play, *Gentlemen of the Press*, was based upon the
after-midnight outbursts of Pegler as we sat side by side on
the night rewrite desk in Nassau Street. He had passed his
peak at the time, much of the deftness had gone from his
writing since his Chicago days, but he was definitely fascinating when he went into one of his tirades, and he believed
every word of it when he asserted that a sports-writing son,
Westbrook, would turn out to be one of the outstanding members of the newspaper profession.

I found the *Tribune's* day desk vague and uncertain, but
there was a great deal of satisfaction in dealings with the
night side. Dwight S. Perrin was a good night city editor,
quick and decisive, and he had an uncommonly perceptive
assistant in B. O. McAnney, friendly, likable, human—and
also fiery—and a man to whom everybody in the shop seemed
to be forever going with their problems. The day desk respected his ability, his straightforwardness, and the sharp-
ness of his news judgments, and they knew that he didn't
scare easily. Staff reporters and rewrite men fairly worshipped
him. Perrin and McAnney were in direct command of a spectacular rewrite battery, whose outstanding men were the un-
assuming and soft-spoken Robert B. Peck and the more
voluble Frederic F. Van de Water, a two-man newspaper, fast
at their typewriters, gifted in composition, and who had the
powers of concentration and endurance. The Peck–Van de

Water team was held in reverence by the entire *Tribune* organization.

Bob Peck would report for work in Nassau Street around 5:30 or 6 P.M., coming over from his home in Brooklyn, and would sit at his typewriter for a good seven or eight hours—unhurried, unemotional, and seemingly unaware of his perfection at his job. I believe that the only time he was ever sent out on an assignment was on the day of the Wall Street explosion. He sauntered down into the area of the Subtreasury Building, made a few notes at the scene of death and destruction, chatted with other staff members who had been assigned to the story, glanced over the countless strips of city-news copy, talked quietly with the night desk—and went to his typewriter and turned out a masterpiece. And then there was the night of the advent of prohibition. Boyden Sparkes was assigned to write the story of the coming of the great drought to Broadway, and he spent hours in his quest of color copy, making many of the gaudier spots in the Great White Way area between Times Square and Reisenweber's at Columbus Circle. He charged back into the office, conferred quickly with Night City Editor Perrin, and went to his desk to turn out a star reporter's account of New York going dry. But he made the mistake of picking up a first edition and reading the piece Bob Peck had dashed off in an hour, and without leaving the *Tribune* building. He read on and on and stood transfixed. He went back to the night desk. "No use," he said. "Peck has told it all and I'd be a fool to try to improve upon it." Then he tore his notes into bits.

I was fairly overwhelmed, as a young and impressionable

newcomer upon the New York scene, by the skill of Peck & Van de Water in their high-speed rewriting skill; by the finesse of Boyden Sparkes in his coverage of the big stories; by the ability of the elfinlike Ishbel Ross, small, shy, and quiet, who would merely copy the city news ticker material, word for word, if they assigned her to deadly day rewrite, but who wrote beautifully and imaginatively when they sent her out on a story worth her time.

I was present when the hulking and sapient Heywood Broun, dramatic critic, shuffled off to the *World* for better pay, and when Percy Hammond, fretful, confused, frightened, definitely unsure of himself in a new setup after long and distinguished years of Chicago play reviewing, arrived to take up his Broadway stand. He did his writing in the composing room in his early Nassau Street years, being discovered there by Bo McAnney, who immediately got him a desk upstairs. It probably occurred to McAnney later that he had spoiled Percy's feeling of martyrdom and had also exposed him to the gibes of Burton Rascoe, the paper's book critic. They apparently had brought along their Cook County feud when they came on to New York.

The post of managing editor of a newspaper, as we had come to know it in the South, was a job of more or less permanence. Once a man got it he held it until he died or retired or moved on to the editorship. But things worked differently in the North. There was no security at all in being appointed to the post at the *Tribune*. Gentlemen who held it came along, and vanished, in a bewildering procession.

The *Tribune's* publisher, Ogden Reid, was something of

an *opera bouffe* character, who would fall asleep at his desk night after night while a taxi, with its clock running, waited for him at the Nassau Street curb. But there were fine things about Ogden Reid: he had a great sense of fairness, he was quick to correct an injustice, he was a good deal of a balance wheel in spite of his seeming indifference, and he seldom hesitated when an important decision had to be made. Also, his judgments were generally sound, his foresightedness frequently astonishing to his associates. Many of those who worked for him thought something went out of the stability of the *Tribune* when he died.

No young man coming into New York from the southland or the midlands along about 1920–1921 and taking up big-time newspaper work could have failed to be conscious of the readability of Burton Rascoe (who became the wildest dramatic critic Broadway has ever known) in his writing about books and authors; of the all-around ability of such general reporters as Edwin C. Hill, Jack Winkler, Gene Fowler, Don Clark, and Walter Davenport. Herbert Asbury, who quit the city room to make real money with his book writing, had the speed of a professional stenographer when he hammered a typewriter at the rewrite desk. Don Skene was dramatic critic of a paper in Oregon, and the severity of his review of Otis Skinner's performance in *The Honor of the Family* cost him his job. The agent for the show went to Skinner about it. "You know he was right," the agent said. "It was a lousy performance." Skinner was contrite. He became so upset he brought Skene to New York with the company, and Skene immediately went to work for the *Tribune*.

There was every kind of man in the multitude of editorial workers in the New York newspaper field before the great shrinkage of metropolitan dailies began, before Frank A. Munsey began buying them up, buying them out, and killing them off. Gilman Parker, gigantic of frame and a good reporter, a fellow of unsuspected morbidity, went to his death as a suicide. So did John Monk Saunders, who seemed to have everything. Saunders lived in a beautiful Central Park South apartment, which cost much more than he earned as a reporter. But he was seemingly a man with money of his own; he was a Rhodes scholar and an athlete, handsome and gentlemanly, was well liked by his associates, and he could talk with fluency and authority on the subjects of books, art, poetry, sculpture, archaeology, and world travel. Women found him irresistible and he was told by many of them that he was good-looking enough to be an actor. It was the general opinion of most of us that he wouldn't stay long in newspaper work and that he would probably become a Hollywood executive. Well, he did go to the coast after a period with the *American* magazine and he did get into the $1000-a-week class as a screen writer. There were later reports that things weren't going so well for him. Finally, a brief news dispatch bearing a Florida date line gave the news that he had hanged himself.

Charlie McGill was a bright-faced fellow who eventually took himself away from the rat race of the big time to go in for the comparative peace (with some hysteria thrown in) of being an executive of a Connecticut daily. Charlie, when I got to know him early in the prohibition era, talked of two things: the girl at Natick, Massachusetts, to whom he was engaged, and a plan for getting rich quick. It was his notion that there'd be a lot of money in buying up cases of right-off-the-boat liquor at Providence at reasonable prices, bringing it to New York, and selling it to friends at the regular city-wide bootleg price, which was around six dollars per bottle for bathtub gin. I went in on the scheme with Charlie—he had put up the capital with a thousand dollars from a savings account, something unusual indeed for a $55-a-week man—and I helped him store the supplies in an apartment in the Fifties, near Fifth Avenue. There was a brisk demand for our supplies, right from the beginning, but the great majority of our customers, fellow newspapermen, wanted their goods on credit, and at the end of three months Charlie took an accounting and found that we were $487 in the red and down to our last twenty bottles. "Let's drink up what we have left," he said, "and let's go out of business. I don't think we'll ever collect what is owed us." We never did.

It was my general idea, in coming to New York, that I would try to establish myself as a reporter in the field of city-desk assignments and gradually return to playwrighting, a passion of teen-age years. Somehow, during the excitement of Atlanta, my playwrighting got rudely sidetracked. My activity as a staff reporter in New York suddenly ceased when those able and ingratiating fellows, Perrin and McAnney, suggested that I come to work for them on the night rewrite. I took up the new work and enjoyed it. The pay was better, the Peck–Van de Water competition was stimulating, and I somehow found myself with enough energy at the end of my shift, around

1 A.M., to stay on at my desk for another hour or so and work on a short story or a second act.

Then, later, I gave up completely and for all time the thought of becoming a news reporter in the great tradition when the chance came to get into the dramatic department. I grabbed it. From the very moment I shifted operations to the drama coop and began writing of Broadway I seceded from the city room; I was in on a racket. I was then a specialist; I was taking up the soft life of a theatrical columnist. I was walking out on everything for which I had been trained and was saying good-by to the front page. Well, perhaps there would be compensations. It might lead to being a dramatic critic for a season or two before I died; I might get a play read by an important manager and then produced. I've often wondered how I would have fared if I had said, "The hell with all that; I came to New York to be a newspaperman. I want to cover the biggest stories in the world and whether I get a by-line or not. I'm sticking to the city room! I'm a reporter and I don't want to be any damn thing else."

By the time I turned to writing of the theater in the midtwenties I was well on the way to becoming a New Yorker. That's a process that can be extended over a period of several years; my own transition took on momentum when I became a part of the Broadway scene. Once a newcomer in the big town has mastered the complexities of the subway and has been toughened by its bad manners, once he has learned to follow the green line in the below-ground maze of the Grand Central and can give out rudeness as well as take it, he is doomed. He will soon walk a little faster, he will drop most of his Georgia drawl or his Nebraska twang before he knows it, his letters to friends back home will gradually cease, and he will forget to call upon Johnny Fowler at the home-town paper stand in Times Square.

I don't know that taking to living in New York hotels and taking to prohibition gin contributed greatly to the Manhattanizing in my own case, but I do know that I had undergone, by 1925, something of a transformation. Some of my deep-South politeness had vanished; I wasn't any quicker in movement, but was just a little more terse in speech; I had acquired something of the look-out-for-yourself-because-God-won't-do-it-for-you attitude. I was following green lines, squeezing through subway doors, holding my seat as women stood, and was accepting watery Coca-Colas without ice and making little or no fuss about it. By 1925 I would have seemed something of a stranger, if not actually a monstrosity, in the Atlanta scene.

## chapter seven

~~~~~~~~~~

THE NEW YORK stage was moving toward its peak years when the 1920s began. New dramatists, with Eugene O'Neill dominating the field, were coming in upon the Broadway scene. New playhouses were being built, new producing firms were being organized, and some of the producers of the old school, managerial giants of the century's first two decades, were on their way out. Stock companies, which had been scattered so plentifully throughout the land, were beginning to disappear; the theater of the road was diminishing, and in the City of New York, the drama's citadel, the theater was tumultuous.

There was money around in the twenties. Theatrical managers had it and spent it. They bought plays they liked, cast them without difficulty, went into rehearsal, and didn't seem to mind at all if a play's opening was in conflict with those of two or three other productions. The legitimate theater, as the third decade of the twentieth century began, was unchallenged as the foremost medium of the nation's entertainment. Radio was something for the future years; television was

117

as remote as flights to the moon. The talkies were seven or eight years away. Silent pictures had helped to kill off many stock companies and were being shown in many across-America theaters that had been strongholds of the legitimate, but in the delirious midtown area of Manhattan that bears the all-inclusive name of "Broadway" the living theater, the flesh-and-blood drama, was triumphant.

In the early twenties New York presented the spectacle of more than fifty plays running simultaneously; the total was swelled to an extraordinary seventy or so as the years went along, and if there had been theaters to house them, one hundred stage plays would have been available in the nightmarish theatrical district, extending for twenty-odd blocks from north to south and three to four from east to west. Plays weren't hard to get because people were writing them—dramatists of standing, dramatists who were hacks at their trade, dramatists who were just beginning. Plays weren't difficult to produce because a one-set play could be done for five thousand dollars or less and smash-hit notices weren't a positive necessity to obtain a moderate and profitable run. The cut-rate theater ticket was, at the time, an established New York commodity; many plays stayed on for months with the aid of the Joe Leblang cut-rate agency, which did an extraordinary business in the basement of a drugstore at Broadway and 43d Street.

The southernmost margin of New York's theatertown, at the time I reached New York, was around 39th Street and the district extended to 63d Street; the Century Theater, which had begun its career as the ill-fated New in 1909, was still in business at 63d and Central Park West. There was professional theater also in Sheridan Square, 'way downtown, at the northern fringes of Greenwich Village, and playgoing was then such a popular pastime for the masses that the Shubert-Riviera found a steady week-to-week clientele at Broadway and 96th Street. There was also drama in Brooklyn and the Bronx. Nearby Stamford, in Connecticut, was regarded by the producers as being extraordinarily desirable as a tryout town, second only to Atlantic City, and many productions played pre-Broadway engagements in such New Jersey resort communities as Long Branch and Asbury Park.

I was working on the night rewrite desk at the *New York Tribune* when the twenties began. I had one night off weekly —the five-day week for newspapermen was something then undreamed of—and I got into the theaters by paying for my seats, generally getting them from the Leblang agency. But when I saw the hits, such as the *Ziegfeld Follies* and *Clarence* and John Drinkwater's *Abraham Lincoln* and the immortal *Rain*, I was in a far-back balcony perch. Leblang didn't handle those tickets. They were obtainable only by going to the box office, queuing up, and doing so well in advance. I was never able to see *all* the plays—nobody could when they were coming along at the rate of two hundred and more a season, as compared with the sixty to seventy totals of two decades later— but my playgoing always included at least one matinee performance a week and, as a paying customer and before I began going to the theater on press seats, I don't believe that I missed one important play that had an engagement of more than a month.

When not engaged in the labors of night rewrite I was on assignments from the city desk and found great excitement in wandering about New York, in getting to know it. I was sent several times to cover the new bill at the Palace, the number one vaudeville house in America, and was almost tearful in my joy upon being told to go to the Hotel Ambassador and talk to George M. Cohan, whose violent personal participation in the actors' strike, on the side of the managers, the strike which the actors won, had left him a bitter man. Staff assignments took me several times to the gaudy Hotel Knickerbocker, which towered at 42d Street and Broadway; to the old and ornate Waldorf-Astoria at 34th Street and Fifth Avenue, and to the Hotel Belmont on 42d Street, another distinguished landmark that was doomed. I had difficulty holding my cup when the great Minnie Maddern Fiske poured tea for me at the Murray Hill, and I sat transfixed at Childs at 2 A.M. when David Belasco, with his chalk-white face, his turn-around collar, and trailed by his deferential entourage, took a table twenty feet away and ordered wheat cakes and coffee.

The Great Transition, brought on by the advent of prohibition, was under way as I took up my life in New York. Such famous establishments as Rector's, Churchill's, Jack's, Shanley's, Reisenweber's, the Hotel Knickerbocker, and Delmonico's were bowing out, the victims of prohibition. Speakeasies, thousands of them, were coming in. Grover A. Whalen was forever in the news, as was Mayor Hylan; the scandal of the Chicago Black Sox was about to break. Idaho's redoubtable Senator Borah was in the headlines with great frequency, as were Senator Lodge and Carter Glass and Rose Pastor Stokes and Trotsky and Emma Goldman and Samuel Gompers. There was no more colorful showman in the world than Morris Gest, who was already talking of bringing over the Moscow Art Theater. Sinclair Lewis emerged from the pack with the writing of *Main Street.* Jeanne Eagels distinguished herself in *Rain,* and Alfred Lunt, from out of the stock companies, served notice on all of Broadway that a new and extraordinary personality had moved in upon the theatrical scene.

Billy Guard, press man for the Metropolitan Opera, was widely known in the New York scene, as was Gatti-Casazza, for whom he worked. Enrico Caruso, living at the Hotel Vanderbilt after moving from the Knickerbocker, was in uncertain health, but he was still the Met's greatest star. John McCormack was a redoubtable figure in the concert field, as were Galli-Curci and Emmy Destinn. The Met's Geraldine Farrar had gained a new fame in the silent pictures, and was in the top-star category along with such people as William S. Hart, Constance Talmadge, and Gloria Swanson. I got to the opera only three or four times during those early New York years, but frequently saw Billy Guard, a friend since his Atlanta invasions, and who frequently went into a blasting of my prefence of the theater to grand opera.

I went to Reisenweber's once or twice just before it passed into oblivion, was taken to Joel's by the hulking and gifted Heywood Broun, had lunch several times at the Knickerbocker, was invited by the fabulous Morris Gest to the Hunting Room of the Astor, lunchtime meeting place of the rich and famous theatrical managers, and spent many afternoons watching the big-league baseball games. I'd often heard Savannahians talk of the great Ty Cobb and of his exploits with the Augusta team of the South Atlantic League; Cobb was now making regular visits to New York with the Detroit Tigers. Not so fast as he had been but still a terrific hitter, he put on a show for me one afternoon by getting five hits in succession. I was a witness of some of Babe Ruth's prodigious feats during his first season with the Yankees, and I had a seat far out in the lower right-field grandstand when one of Carl Mays's under-hand fast balls struck the hard-hitting Cleveland shortstop, Ray Chapman, in the head. Chapman dropped as if he had been shot. He was carried from the field, never to regain con-sciousness, and died early the next afternoon.

I liked New York from the very beginning. I liked the din and the pace and the throb of it, the sights and the sensa-tions that were available for five cents—a ride upon the screech-ing and frightening el trains; a ferry trip to Staten Island, af-fording the view of the lower-Manhattan skyscrapers, huddled together in all their magnificence; the ride all the way to Coney Island, with the enticements of Luna Park and Steeple-chase waiting at the end of the line; the trip to the Bronx zoo; and the ferry rides to the Jersey shore, to Weehawken and the Palisades. One of the first assignments I had in New York was that of covering a dinner in Chinatown's twisting Doyers Street; the piece was printed precisely as written, and Chinatown held its place in my affections from that time on. I enjoyed strolling along the Bowery and going to the tip of Manhattan, at the Battery, to enjoy a waterfront scene that had more bustle than the Savannah River afforded. I'm sure that I got lost in the subway as often as any newcomer to New York ever did, but the sheer speed of it fascinated me, and there was always some satisfaction in displaying my knowledge of the underground to visitors. When I left Atlanta I knew it street by street, all the way into the surrounding suburbs. Within a year or so after arriving in New York I knew Manhattan's geography as well as any native ever did but was never sure of myself in Brooklyn. The Bronx will always remain an uncharted and mysterious area. Just across that narrow river and I can lose my way quickly, as quickly as I might in Pittsburgh or Bombay.

In 1920 I was paid $60 weekly by the *New York Tribune,* earned extra money by writing for the Sunday magazine, a bit more for contributions to Southern dailies, and managed to sell short pieces of fiction from time to time. I lived on Haven Avenue, far uptown and near the frozen margins of the Hudson, during my first winter in New York, sub-zero for much of the time, and later moved to Morningside Heights and the Columbia University area, which seemed semitropical by comparison. For some months I tried a walk-up at 50th Street near Fifth Avenue and lived for some time in Pomander Walk, that charming row of houses running through from 94th to 95th Street, and to the west of Broadway. When I lived at 120th Street and the cobbled Amsterdam Avenue I burrowed into the subway at 116th Street and Broadway, stayed underground until I reached Park Place, at City Hall Park, doing my reading by electric light on the roaring trains, at my home in a court apartment in the Poinciana, and at my desk at 154 Nassau Street. There are many New York nightworkers who go along for years, I suppose, without seeing any daylight at all.

By 1923—at least, during 1923—I was enjoying comparative wealth, achieved by the mere trick of working sixteen hours daily, taking on the side-line job of operating a New York office for the *Atlanta Journal* in the Hotel Astor from 10 A.M. to 6 P.M., and then reporting at the *Tribune* for a shift that ran until 1 A.M., at times until 2. Late in 1924 I got into the *Tribune's* dramatic department, shifting over from the night city desk, and my life and my world changed overnight. My job became the theater, which I had loved since boyhood. The people I saw daily were the people of the theater—the players, the producers, the playwrights. My theatergoing was now intensified; I got to seeing six, sometimes seven, plays weekly instead of two, and always on tickets that were presented with the compliments of the managements.

During the first year or so after taking on the Broadway run I kept expecting to come upon an old fellow of stately tread and regal bearing and greatly in need of a haircut, and say, "Why, hello there, Mr. Richmond!" and then become engaged in a wonderfully sentimental reunion with my old friend from Virginia travels. But there was never a glimpse of him on any street or in any play. I did, however, see Broadway performances of many players who had come through the South in road plays. And, as I wrote of the theater daily, got to meet and to know numerous road stars who had played engagements at the Savannah Theater and the Atlanta.

I was frequently jolted by the perceptible aging that a

decade had brought to erstwhile ingenues and leading women of touring attractions and certainly could not fail to notice that most of the actors who had come to my town were seemingly unmarked by the passing of years. James Rennie was as youthful-looking in *Moonlight and Honey-suckle* as he had been ten years before in a Savannah stock production of *Sauce for the Goose*. The Lynne Overman of *Just Married* was an actor unchanged, just as blithe as he had been when he played Savannah in *The Wolf*, and when I was introduced to John Drew at the time he was in Rupert Hughes's *The Cat-Bird* he was the same Drew, in looks, manner, and intonation, who had come a-trouping through Dixie in Somerset Maugham's *Smith*.

As to the ravages of time upon the fairer sex, I was quite dismayed, and probably showed it, when I was presented to a character actress, shrunken and worn, who was a glamorous stock star when I first gazed upon her. I was stunned to be told, at a tea at the Little Church Around the Corner, that the little lady over in a corner, now something of an invalid, was the woman who had enchanted the Georgia critics when she had come down our way as the singing and dancing star of a popular musical comedy.

Names of some of the touring players I'd seen in my Bull Street playgoing had left such an imprint upon my memory that I often took great pains to track them down in the North, and those little reunions sometimes afforded great pleasure— and now and then brought on disillusionment. There was the case of Thomas Coffin Cooke, who had given what seemed to me a remarkably effective performance in Eugene Walter's

*Paid in Full.* I was told that he was stage-managing the Broadway production of *The Constant Nymph* and called backstage to introduce myself and to tell him how good I thought he had been in the role of Joe Brooks, the embezzler-husband. "Yeah," he said, "and thanks very much—but that was all in the past. Now, if you don't mind, will you get the hell out front? Visitors are not allowed backstage."

During lunch one day with George M. Cohan at his upper Fifth Avenue apartment I was talking of the actors who had come South in Cohan & Harris productions and remarked that one of the most engaging comedy performances Savannah had ever seen was that of Fred Niblo playing the John Barrymore part in a touring company of Winchell Smith's *The Fortune Hunter.* Cohan listened and was silent for a moment. Then he said, "Listen, kid. Wonder if you'll do me a favor. Don't ever mention Niblo's name to me again. It's a name we don't like to hear in this house. We are no longer friends."

I got to seeing Edward Arnold frequently after reaching New York, liked him a great deal, talked with him of his being stranded in Savannah with the Liberty Theater stock company, and had difficulty in restraining him from paying out of his own pocket the money the company owed me for general services when the Georgia engagement ended. He contributed a bit of philosophy: "Perhaps it's a good thing that you didn't get paid. It taught you at an early stage that the theater is a fascinating business—and damned precarious."

David Warfield invited me to lunch at his apartment in Central Park West, spoke of his feeling for the beauty of

Savannah—he'd played there in *The Music Master*—and said that when he realized a great ambition, that of playing Shylock in *The Merchant of Venice,* he would probably retire from the stage (he did, too).

When the musical play *Alma, Where Do You Live?* reached Savannah I saw the opening matinee performance from a gallery seat and was so fascinated by the playing and singing of Nanette Flack, the statuesque leading woman, I returned to the gallery for the evening performance. I had no luck at all in getting to see Miss Flack backstage, but after I had been in the North for some years I wrote to her, received an immediate reply, and called upon her at her home in Flushing and had an enchanting visit as she went through the entire score of *Alma, Where Do You Live?*

Jeanne Eagels, at the time I met her in Atlanta on an interview assignment, was a fascinating woman. She was even more glamorous, quite a good deal more overpowering, when I got to know her in New York, and by this time, through her performance in *Rain,* she had established herself as a great actress. I was having dinner in a small, charming restaurant, Le Mirliton, in New York's East 58th Street, between Fifth and Madison Avenues, when she came in and sat at an adjoining table. She asked if I lived in the neighborhood, and I told her I had an apartment directly overhead—a third-floor walk-up. She said she neded such a place in just such a neighborhood and demanded that I go up with her immediately and show my quarters. Just what she wanted, she decided; she was weary of driving to her Westchester home every night in the week; she must have a flat in town. Two weeks later there was circuslike commotion in my block as Miss Eagels, having rented an apartment on the floor just below me, arrived with her entourage—cook, maid, and chauffeur. She was happy and excited. She'd found just the hideaway she'd been seeking; she'd save Westchester for week ends. Within a month there were callers in such profusion in 58th Street that Miss Eagels found herself fleeing in desperation back to Westchester to find a bit of peace.

I first saw Tallulah Bankhead when she was playing on Broadway in a meretricious drama, *The Exciters*—she was throaty and alluring and entirely unbelievable—but I did not meet her until 1930, when she was playing *Camille* in London. She had become a London star with genuine box-office power and she was cordial, hearty, and explosive when I called upon her in her dressing room. She told me, huskily, to ask my questions, that she had exactly five minutes, and she was sure I wouldn't mind if she undressed completely as we went along with the interview. The disrobing was all right, I said, but I needed an hour or so. Five minutes wouldn't do for the Bankhead-Conquers-London sort of piece I wanted to send back to the *New York Sun*. She glared at me and then she roared, "Difficult, eh? . . . All right, Southern boy. You get the hell over to my house in Farm Street after to-night's performance and I'll talk to you all night."

I got to Farm Street at midnight, waited for her until 3 A.M., and then, as she sat on the floor and was rather steadily disconcerting because she wasn't wearing pants, I made jottings on a pad for two hours and sent back two thousand words to New York on her views on love, marriage, sex, London, New York, Hollywood, and the universe. I shall always remember Tallulah's final words as she saw me to the door, "I don't care what you write about me, but for Christ sake make me out as having a sense of humor!"

I'd always heard that the women of the theater who became stars for Belasco were more or less hypnotized by him and saw some evidence of this at a party at the home of Lenore Ulric during her triumphant run in *Lulu Belle*. For several hours Miss Ulric, seemingly unaware of the presence of a house full of guests, sat at the feet of the great D. B., gazing upon him with her beautiful eyes, and listening with nothing less than rapture to his murmurings to those who came past his chair in a steady procession all evening.

One actress who somehow resisted the Belasco hypnosis was the forthright Katharine Cornell, who starred for him in *Tiger Cats*. Miss Cornell, in talking with me later of her engagement, summed it all up in this fashion, "Mr. Belasco didn't understand me and I didn't understand him." This was some time after Miss Cornell had captivated New York with her performance in *A Bill of Divorcement* and after I had gone to her dressing room at the Times Square Theater with such a naive and awkward question as "Have you any thoughts on marriage, Miss Cornell?" I shall never forget the amused look that she gave me or how deflated I was when she said ever so calmly, "No thoughts at all, but I *am* married."

Miriam Hopkins, Georgia-born, was one of my close friends for years; she was in plays that were good, bad, and atrocious. There was always considerable drama in her personal life, more than a bit of melodrama the night that a

playwright, Patrick Kearney, who had made the dramatization of Theodore Dreiser's *An American Tragedy*, reached
for a butcher knife and chased her out of her house and down
a street in Greenwich Village. Mr. Kearney committed suicide
a year or so later. Miss Hopkins, a creature of impulse and
emotion, once threw a diamond-studded wrist watch from
the twentieth floor of the Hotel Pierre during a quarrel with
the man who gave it to her and tossed a tie clasp of mine
from an even higher floor of the Hotel Lincoln just because
she didn't like the design. Two hours later a platinum clasp,
with rubies in it, arrived at my room from Tiffany's. She was
always one to whom money came easily, and she never regarded it as sacred. She liked buying things for friends. I was
with her the evening in Hollywood when she walked into
a car lot where new trailers were for sale. She bought one
within five minutes and paid an extra fifty dollars to get it
delivered at the moment to a man with whom she'd been
having dates.

I enjoyed something of a best-friend relationship with
Miriam Hopkins, but even so, there were times when she
became annoyed with me. During such a period she made
a point of not inviting me to a big party she was giving for
theater and screen people. The next day, a little jittery and
more than a little contrite, she mailed me a check for three
thousand dollars as her investment in a play of mine, *Miss
Quis*. After returning with a husband from an elopement to
Maryland she told him that her beautiful home in New York's
Sutton Place was his workshop for the rest of his life (he was
a writer, and writers belonged to her pattern), but when she

grew tired of the marriage—and of him—she knew of no way to get him out of the house except to move out herself, and then rent it. This she did.

Miriam Hopkins was never one to go along with moderate means; she was either desperately broke or bountifully rich. I once met her down the bay when she was aboard an incoming liner with her second or third husband and she cried, "Oh, darling—I'm *so* glad. Have you got $20? We haven't five cents to do any tipping." Sometime later she had to have $1000 immediately and at once and asked me to sign a note. I said that I'd do so, and gladly. "I have an idea," she said. "I'll get another co-maker and perhaps I can get $2000." Then she went to Bennett Cerf, writer and publisher—and the Morris Plan Bank gave her $2000. It was on a previous occasion that she had swept into the city room of the *New York Sun,* clad in a full-length squirrel coat and with her thick blond hair in golden ringlets, dazzling everybody in sight. "Oh, darling," she whispered, "I've *got* to have $5000. The only man I know who has it is Otto Kahn. I'm on my way to see him in Wall Street; I have a taxi waiting. May I use *The Sun's* telephone?" She made her call, reached Mr. Kahn, got an appointment, and came back an hour later—and in the same cab—with a check for $1250. "Mr. Kahn," she said, "is a conservative man; he thought this was all I'd need to pay my bills. And he said he wants to keep a friend; he wants me to pay him back." She paid him back.

Then, at another time, and when she was fairly overwhelmed by the money she was getting from the cinema, she asked me to take her to dinner in Hollywood and said that she would then treat me to an hour or so at a nearby gambling casino. The dinner cost me $28.75; our time at the roulette and dice tables cost her several hundred. It was during this stay in Hollywood—I was there on a leave of absence from *The Sun,* writing a picture at the Universal Studios—that a rented car I was driving got out of control on a steep hill, tore down and on across Santa Monica Boulevard, and crashed into a filling station, knocking down a gas pump and upsetting things generally. The next day, before litigation set in, Miss Hopkins came around with her checkbook. She wrote out a check for five hundred dollars. "Here, darling," she said, handing it to me, "pay the little man for that filling station—and get on back to New York. It's safer for you there."

I've known actresses who liked their food and their drink, too. Peggy Wood collaborated with me in making a revision of the second act of my small-town play, *Miss Quis,* and her room-service dinners at the Westchester Country Club for two or three weeks cost me  as much as I received in royalties during the first week of the New York run. Miss Wood ordered prodigious mounds of food, ate it all, and without interrupting her own continuous and diverting flow of chatter.

I've always been of the impression that the late Laurette Taylor had a genius for acting surpassed by no other player, living or dead. It was after Miss Taylor had reestablished herself at the top of her profession, through her magnificent performance in *The Glass Menagerie,* that I went with her to dinner at New York's Hotel Sherry-Netherland. It was 6:30, and she wasn't due at the theater for more than an hour. She ordered a cocktail, a stinger before her meal, and that seemed all right. When she asked for a second I was a little surprised, and when she insisted upon a third I became alarmed. "Listen, Miss Taylor," I said, "you're in the greatest success of your career and that's not an easy role you're playing and you've got to play it tonight." "Sure have," she said, "but I'll have another stinger and then I'll eat." She didn't eat; I couldn't get her to the playhouse until she'd finished stinger number 4, but she was as good as ever in her performance that night. She went through without a slip.

I've put in many hours of my life in trying to see Maude Adams. There was that early pursuit of her during reportorial days in Savannah and Atlanta. She was out of the theater during the entire decade of the twenties but when she returned to the stage in 1931, opening a road tour of *The Merchant of Venice* in Cleveland, I went to that city for the first performance. Later, in Los Angeles, I was formally introduced to her and, upon the completion of her cross-America tour, saw her several times in New York. She always knew that I was with a newspaper, but the subject of an interview was never mentioned, I never dared take out a pencil, and she never admitted that she ever saw anything I ever wrote from these meetings. Two or three times, over tea and cakes at New York's Colony Club, where she gets her mail and from which she receives great consideration and protection, Miss Adams talked with me of a play I was writing, but I was always so completely enchanted with her, so delighted to be in her presence, I scarcely heard her suggestions for the improvement of a second act, for the resolving of a third. I found her to be a woman of humor, wisdom, and graciousness, with keen interest in world affairs, a sharp understanding of American politics, and never inclined to go into a recital of adventures, mishaps, and triumphs of her years in the theater. I have never been able to get Miss Adams to have tea with me in my own home or in any place other than the Colony Club, have never been able to make an engagement with her to go to the theater, and have come to know that a particularly pleasant meeting with her is likely to be followed by a six months' interlude of mystery and silence. If she can ever be induced to visit me at my hotel she will find, in a place of great prominence, a painting of her in her suit of leaves from James M. Barrie's enduring *Peter Pan.* It's been a treasured possession since my Atlanta days.

## *chapter eight*

~~~~~~~~~

I GOT to know many dramatic critics, playwrights, and producers of the New York scene after my trans-
fer to the dramatic department of the *Herald Tribune* in
1924, and by the time I began working for the *New York
Sun* in the fall of '26—blissful, crowded, and profitable were
all those years on that great afternoon daily—I was welcome
at the homes of critics, dramatists, and men who put on the
Broadway plays.

I was never on a social basis, exactly, with the strange,
testy, talented, and frequently monstrous Alexander Woollcott, but called on him several times at his East River retreat,
Wit's End. I had the good judgment to turn down an invita-
tion to visit him on his island in Vermont, was insulted by
him several times, and befriended by him at least twice. There
was the time of a big theater party, for which dinner jackets
were required. The shirt I wore wasn't a good fit and my
black tie wouldn't stay in place, but I didn't believe that such
imperfections would be noticed in the big crush. Woollcott's

135

eye, however, spotted my rebellious shirt front and he found it a cause for mirth and for whispers to the woman beside him. I became confused, tripped, spilled my champagne, and decided that Mr. A. W. was the prize sonofabitch of the world when he became convulsed with laughter. A few weeks later, on an opening night, I raced up the aisle at the fall of the curtain and reached the sidewalk only to find Woollcott at the curb. I went up to him and said, "Good evening." "Good evening," he said stiffly, "and, let me also add, good-by. I don't intend to stand here for the next ten minutes and have you pretend to be my equal." He walked twenty feet and joined Robert Benchley.

He could be that vile. He often was. There was a bigness about him, too. On the evening of the day I had applied to Gilbert Gabriel for a job in the dramatic department of *The Sun* Woollcott saw Gabriel at the theater. He crossed to the other side of the house and spoke to Gabriel. "Ward More-house tells me he wants to go to work for you. Take him. He's a good man." And then, several years later, when Woollcott was told I was sailing for London, he sat down at his type-writer in Boston and wrote a witty guest column for me. "You'll be busy," he said, "having a final drink and saying good-by to a lot of people who hope they'll never see you again. Perhaps a thousand words will help you in the last minute rush." They certainly did.

Woollcott had a way of getting half a day's work done by 10 A.M. as he sat about his pine-paneled East River apart-ment in his silk pajamas, drinking pots of hot coffee and sip-ping orange juice. On several visits I found him caustic and insulting, and at other times he was hospitable and enormously entertaining. There was a particularly gray morning when he sat beside a window watching a fussy tug as it churned its way past Wit's End. "I like to sit here," he murmured absent-mindedly. "Just sit here and watch the big boats and the little boats and the dead bodies go by. Those bodies generally make about ten knots an hour." A moment of silence and he was having more coffee and was talking about actors and the drama and such: "Just suppose I'd been in darkest Africa for a dozen years, or had been lost at the headwaters of the Amazon, living off wild berries and monkey meat, and suddenly returned to New York. I'd have to decide, as I came up the bay, what actress I'd want to see on my very first night in town—what one actress beyond all others. Well, that actress would be Ruth Gordon. I like to watch her as I enjoyed watching Mrs. Fiske and Emily Stevens. But if I had a stock company and would have to see this company from day to day and from week to week my actress would be Helen Hayes and my leading man Alfred Lunt."

Then, over more coffee and as a sand scow went by, the articulate Woollcott would switch to such comment as this: "Dramatic critics are honest. They're nice fellows. They write what they think. The trouble is, they don't know a damn thing about the theater. . . . But the critics are the only representatives of civilized, decent American life that you find in the first-night audiences that we have today. Where, in all the world, can you get a gathering as dreary, as ruthless, as moronic as you do at a Broadway opening? First nights have lost their charm and flavor. I never go any more; I won't sit in that company. A première used to be a pleasant occasion; it has now become an unbearable one."

I spent many pleasant and stimulating hours in the company of such dramatists as Channing Pollock and Owen Davis, Winchell Smith and Samuel Shipman, Eugene Walter and Eugene O'Neill and Arthur Wing Pinero.

Owen Davis, a New Englander with considerable Yankee caution and conservatism, a college man and a family man, turned to the theater, of all things, when he got out of Harvard and he's made playwrighting a life's work. He wrote tawdry thrillers with machine-like precision; he stuck to the writing of melodramas intended for the popular-price circuit until along about 1910 when he changed his ways and made the Broadway theater his objective. He went along tirelessly, got many productions, did some first-rate plays—such as *Icebound* and *The Detour* and *The Nervous Wreck* and *The Great Gatsby*—and others that didn't please him or anybody else, and he made a great deal of money. To Davis, one-time author of *Convict 999* and *Tracked around the World*, playwrighting was a full-time job. He was at his desk early every morning and in the course of a day his penciled scrawl would fill many pages with dialogue. He worked swiftly and frequently finished a full-length play in a month or six weeks. His dramatization of F. Scott Fitzgerald's *The Great Gatsby* was done in about three weeks. When he brought down his final curtain he didn't feel that he had earned a holiday for himself and rush off to Nassau or to Capri. He would merely refer to his idea jottings, get out some fresh paper and a collection of sharpened pencils, pull up his chair at his work table, and start all over again, writing, in large and legible letters, ACT ONE, on a glistening sheet.

I met Owen Davis several years after I got to New York and always found him affable, available, and enormously helpful. If you called his uptown hotel and asked, "How's your new play coming along, Mr. Davis?" you could be sure that such a question was quite in order and it would bring forth a leisurely account of his progress. He was always a man of great optimism; he had a capacity for finding new excitement in each new job; he had a way of convincing himself that the play of the moment was the most important of his career.

Channing Pollock was a dramatist with the conversational gift. He believed in himself utterly, he liked to talk of the work he had done and was going to do, and he was equally fascinating in talking to an audience of one across a luncheon table or of hundreds at a women's club. Pollock loved his wife and his daughter, he enjoyed working, he sold many magazine articles and kept many speaking engagements, and when he said that he was a happy man there was conviction in his voice. He believed in himself—and his writings—to such an extent that he refused to accept the adverse verdict of the New York dramatic critics on his play, *The Fool*. His own whirlwind campaign in its behalf—lectures, letters, editorials, curtain talks, impromptu sidewalk sermonizing—turned a potential failure into an emphatic success.

Winchell Smith was a Connecticut Yankee and a practical man of the theater who had a great instinct for the stage.

I saw him frequently in New York, spent several week ends at his beautiful home at Farmington, Connecticut, and heard him tell many stories in connection with his experiences as an usher, as an actor, as a playwright, as a director. He had the sure-fire touch if any dramatist-director ever had; he was author or part author of such smash hits as *Brewster's Millions*, *Polly of the Circus*, *The Fortune Hunter*, *Officer 666*, *The Boomerang*, *Lightnin'*, *Turn to the Right*. He contributed to the writing of many plays without getting billing in the playbills or on the house boards; his directorial magic was of enormous aid to Frederick Lonsdale's *The Last of Mrs. Cheyney*, to Frank Craven's *The First Year*, to Marc Connelly's *The Wisdom Tooth*, and to Paul Osborn's *The Vinegar Tree*. An outspoken, gracious, and modest man, Billy Smith startled me one evening at Farmington when he said, "I've made $3,000,000 from playwrighting, but I've really written only one play. That play was *The Fortune Hunter*. That was mine, from the beginning to the end. All the others were plays that started with somebody else, plays for which another man had the idea, or had done a lot of work and couldn't finish, or plays a manager or an actor or an actress wanted written. . . . Yes, after all those years in this business, going back to *Secret Service*, in which William Gillette gave me a job, I'm still a one-play playwright. Had good sense with *The Fortune Hunter*. Before it opened in New York my wife said, 'Why don't we keep the money from this one? Never touch it, I mean. Just let every cent of it go to the bank and forget it entirely. You will write other plays. We'll spend the money from those.'" Thus *The Fortune Hunter*, a great success,

140

played in New York by John Barrymore and on tour by numerous companies, became the basis of Winchell Smith's playwrighting fortune.

Samuel Shipman was short and thickset, a dramatist with heavy black hair, a fanatical stare, and a ready laugh. He liked to entertain and he was a prodigal host; he enjoyed argument for argument's sake and was always ready to switch from one side to the other in any discussion. If he hadn't turned to playwrighting, which he did in his early years, he would have enjoyed being a trial lawyer; the melodramatics of the courtroom would have appealed to him immensely. He wrote many plays, turning them out swiftly. Many of them were cheap, all of them were more or less mechanical, several of them were adroitly constructed. One of his biggest hits was *East Is West*, done with John B. Hymer, and when it was delivered to the theater-wise William Harris, Jr., that showman read it with increasing interest, chuckled as he went along, and decided that his authors had written an approximation of *Madame Butterfly*. "I didn't want to produce *Madame Butterfly*," he told me later, "so I suggested to the boys that they give it a new twist. They were fellows who could supply any twist you liked and they did the job in Atlantic City over a week end."

During Samuel Shipman's period of great activity—he belonged to the pre-O'Neill years, 1915–1920, years in which artificial drama flourished, in which the "crook play" enjoyed a vogue—he did a great deal of his writing in Atlantic City, which held a great fascination for those of the Broadway world who had the money to enjoy it. Shipman's plays earned money and he spent it freely. He always felt that an Atlantic

City stay from Friday to Monday was just about enough time to do an entire three-act play. He dictated a great deal of his dialogue to a faithful and expert secretary, Pauline Halley (she was forever talking of a bright son, Rudolph, for whom she predicted big things), and when he wasn't engaged in play composition in an ocean-front suite he was at his labors in New York's Hotel Alamac, where he had an apartment, or in his offices in the Times Building, Times Square, where he always maintained open house. He liked visitors; he enjoyed interruptions; he particularly enjoyed calls from gentlemen of the press who were covering the Broadway beat. It was his impression, and one justified by experience, that the boys liked good rye whisky. It was one of Pauline Halley's duties to see that the office decanter was never empty. Shipman—he was always Sammy to the Broadway mob—took his plays seriously and when the critics didn't he often became enraged, but it was anger that vanished as quickly as it came. He never regarded himself as a great playwright, but he did feel that he knew how to write plays that would bring enough people into a theater, and for a sufficient time, to provide money for the manager, for the actors, and himself. Most of his plays did.

The theater, as a result of the blood transfusion it received from Eugene O'Neill and other dramatists of the wonderful twenties, moved on ahead of Sammy Shipman, just as it outgrew other playwrights of the 1910–1920 decade—Eugene Walter, Bayard Veiller, Avery Hopwood, Augustus Thomas. I got to be one of the dynamic Shipman's good friends; I saw Walter, Veiller, and Hopwood from time to time through the

142

years. Walter, author of such pioneering plays as *Paid in Full* and *The Easiest Way*, came to Broadway after years in Hollywood, wandered about town, took me to lunch at the Astor, and remarked ever so sadly, "What the hell has come over this town? Where the hell is everybody? I don't know anybody any more. I miss Jack's and Rector's and the Knickerbocker bar. Nothing for a man like me to do except to get the hell back to California—and fast!"

Bayard Veiller had something of the look of a prize fighter or of a man who might be in a prize fighter's corner. Short and stocky and quick in movement, he was the dramatist who took his place in the Broadway legends when he sold his melodrama, *Within the Law*, outright for three thousand dollars, only to have it turn out to be a million-dollar hit. Veiller, an erstwhile reporter on the *New York World*, was a friendly man. He attended the first-time-on-any-stage performance of my play, *Gentlemen of the Press*, in Connecticut, and came around the next day with detailed suggestions for a new, and far better, final scene. Avery Hopwood, author of *The Gold Diggers* and *Fair and Warmer* and co-author (with Mary Roberts Rinehart) of such tremendously successful pieces as *Seven Days* and *The Bat*, was tall, lean, blond, laconic. I saw him frequently around the Al Woods offices, something of a meeting place for actors, authors, directors, scenic designers, promoters, Broadway reporters, and I went with him several times to a nearby automat for pie alamode, which he liked immensely. He was consuming his second portion of such a dish one afternoon when he told me that his producer had paid Douglas Fairbanks, Sr., $40 a week for playing a part in his comedy, *Clothes*, that he had enjoyed working on the thriller, *The Bat*, more than any work he had ever done. And then he startled me with the mild assertion that, with two or three more plays, he would feel that he had run his course, and he didn't believe that he had more than two or three years of life left to him. Several years later he died of drowning in the Mediterranean.

The tall, gaunt, and carelessly dressed Wilson Mizner, wit, adventurer, Alaskan prospector, had finished his playwrighting career when I came to the North; he had been a part of the Broadway scene in the days of Rector's and Diamond Jim Brady. When I met him he was working as a writer at the Warner Brothers studio in Hollywood. "What a hell of a business for me to be in, the movies," he remarked, "but they're paying me. A man's got to live, I suppose, and this is the shortest cut between here and the grave." I got to know Rachel Crothers at the time she was directing rehearsals of a small-town comedy she had written, *The Book of Charm*. There was a small and vivid role in it, that of a book salesman, and it was the notion of the play's high-powered press agent, one Tom Weatherly, that I should turn actor again and go along with it as a part-time job. "Hell," he said, "there are several hours in the day when you're not working for the *Herald Tribune* and the *Atlanta Journal*. You might as well pick up another sixty bucks a week trying to be an actor." Well, I tried. Miss Crothers regarded me with some doubt as I went into my first reading, but she rehearsed me patiently, line for line. After three days, however, it was our mutual decision that I wasn't glib enough, not professional enough.

"But don't give up yet," she said. "We have another man here. You just stand by and we'll hear him read, and then we'll see how you feel about it." I heard the reading, and I put on my hat. The actor who got the job was Lee Tracy.

I have always been grateful for the few hours I spent in the New York apartment of the brilliant Edward Sheldon, author of numerous plays, whose last years were spent in paralysis and blindness, and whose inspirational words were sought and treasured by those of the theater fortunate enough to gain admittance to his quarters.

I shall also remember always, and down to the last detail, the entire afternoon spent in an upstairs apartment at 116-A Harley Street, London, with Arthur Wing Pinero, of the bushy, fantastic eyebrows, and a man of some fifty plays. He was aging, somewhat deaf, and most of his vitality seemed to be in those eyebrows as he sat in a red-leather chair, smoked cigarette after cigarette, talked hoarsely of his experiences in America and rambled along with such words as: "The American theater, the New York theater—they were always wonderful to me. Gave me as good treatment as I ever got from my native England. Ever so many of my plays have been done in New York. How I wish I'd been there to see Ethel Barrymore in *Mid-Channel*. I wish sometime she would play Paula Tanqueray. . . . I loved my trips to New York, but it's been more than forty years since I was in your great country. I could never go back again—never. I'd be scared to death." . . . A later development: Ethel Barrymore *did* play Paula Tanqueray. Very fine in it, too.

New York newspaper work has taken me on many self-

145

assignments I've cherished. One particularly unforgettable experience was a week end spent in the French chateau of Eugene O'Neill, near Tours, in early April of 1930; another was that of a day with William Gillette, the celebrated actor-playwright-director, at his field stone castle, Seventh Sister, high above the Connecticut River at Hadlyme, Connecticut.

Eugene O'Neill, then forty-one, was living in his great gray château, about a hundred miles from Paris, working on *Mourning Becomes Electra*, wandering about his beautiful wood, taking high-speed spins along the empty roads in his demoniacal Bugatti racer, and greatly enjoying his life abroad. I sat with him for hours before a great open fire in his high-ceilinged living room, and he talked along quietly and fascinatingly of his plays and of the people who had appeared in them. He told me that he had been in too big a hurry in writing *Dynamo*, which failed; that *Mourning Becomes Electra* was his most ambitious undertaking to date; that the play for which he had the greatest affection was *The Great God Brown* and the one into which he had put the best writing was the commercially unsuccessful *Lazarus Laughed*. He had been fortunate, he said, in the choice of the players for his works. Two performances seemed particularly outstanding: Walter Huston, in the role of the grim and God-fearing Ephraim Cabot in *Desire Under the Elms,* Lynn Fontanne as Nina Leeds, that fascinating creature of passion, bitterness, and frustration in his gigantic, nine-act drama, *Strange Interlude.*

William Gillette, a distinguished actor-dramatist, won re-

nown in the nineties for his writing of the Civil War melodrama, *Secret Service*. He went on to create the role of Sherlock Holmes in an adroit dramatization of the A. Conan Doyle
stories. Some of his contemporaries ranted in their performances; Gillette got his effects with a quietly spoken word, with
a shrug, a whisper, a glance. He was a master in the art of
underplaying. He was a man of culture, humor, and great
charm; he was gracious in his letter writing and always used
two kinds of ink, black for the body of his letters and red for
special emphasis. He had had his New York triumphs in *A Successful Calamity* and *Dear Brutus* and, when I met him, along
about 1930, had revived *Sherlock Holmes* to the great delight of everybody. It was sometime later that he invited me
to visit him at his medieval retreat in Connecticut. He was
then living—the year was 1935—as a recluse in his austere
rock pile, living with his Japanese butler, Takizawa, and a
swarm of yellow cats. He also had a great open fireplace and
we put in a morning before it, and he went into chuckling
reminiscence of some of the theater's great people—Charles
Frohman and James M. Barrie, Constance Collier and Marie
Doro, Arthur Hopkins and Helen Hayes and Estelle Win-
wood and George C. Tyler. It was after lunch that he suggested a ride on his private miniature railroad. He was gone
for a few minutes and returned wearing blue overalls, an
engineer's cap, and heavy gloves. He led me to his tiny train,
ready and waiting upon its narrow-gauge tracks, and bade me
step into a passenger compartment. Then he climbed into
the engineer's seat of the undersized locomotive, blew a
whistle, gave the throttle a jerk, and off we went on a 3-mile

ride over tracks that wound through his great estate. When the run was completed and he had graciously assisted me to the home platform, he said, "Now, I think we should go right back into the house, sit down before that fire, and have some nice tea—with rum."

Some ten minutes later I heard his step on the narrow balcony, high above the living room. I turned and saw him. There he stood in a black suit—tall, gray, dignified, impassive—and when he spoke it was in the voice of Mr. Holmes of Baker Street. Tea and rum, he said ever so faintly, would be served almost instantly.

Then, and exactly on cue, one of his doors of chopped oak, with its hand-carved latch, was quietly opened, and Takizawa, the butler, made his smiling and noiseless entrance. William Gillette came slowly down the stairway.

I've said that William Gillette, besides having charm and great ability in the theater, was a man of humor. It was in the early 1930s that, in one of his letters to the Hotel Plaza, asking for a reservation, he made a most specific request, addressed it to the hotel housekeeper, and put it in red ink.

"Will you please," he wrote, "if it is possible in these times of depression, have a wide bed put in my room instead of two narrow ones which usually do duty in your apartments. The time is not far off when I shall have to sleep permanently in very narrow quarters and my wish is not to begin it any sooner than necessary."

Al Woods, one of the most colorful showmen in American theater history, read plays, bought plays, hired actors, booked

148

theaters, talked by telephone to Hollywood, London, and Paris, and smoked expensive cigars as he sat with feet upon his desk in his Eltinge Theater offices. Woods came uptown from the Bowery and the Bowery-style thrillers, adjusted himself to the Broadway theater, and produced a flock of hits. He often had three and four plays running in New York simultaneously, from twenty to thirty companies playing on tour. His office was always a newsy office, always a hangout for newspapermen assigned to the Broadway run. I went to the Eltinge almost daily for years and was more or less certain that the unconquerable Zolotow of *The Times* would show up or that *Variety's* dour and pugnacious and likable Jack Pulaski would be on his way in or out. Stars were forever emerging from the Eltinge's tiny elevator. I remember the afternoon when Al's callers included Claudette Colbert, Jeanne Eagels, Clark Gable, Florence Reed, Lionel Barrymore, and the ultraglamorous Mrs. Leslie Carter, who was to suffer the humiliation of being taken from the cast of *The Shanghai Gesture* after she had played the tryout engagement in Newark. Al Woods was a generous man; he was forever giving his stars gold watches, cases of liquor, salary advances, but he could be good and tough. He didn't dodge a situation that had to be faced. He was always ready to fire an actor if he found he could get a better man; he knew that the illustrious Mrs. Carter wasn't the actress he wanted for the role of Mother Goddam after seeing her give her first performance and sent word to her that she was through with the Newark engagement. He closed the play, to the accompaniment of cheers from a packed house and tears from his star. When

149

he reopened it the younger and more vital Florence Reed was playing Mother Goddam.

Woods once called me in London from Paris and told me to come on over; he wanted to take me to the races and suggested a trip to the south of France via the *Blue Train*. I always liked him, found him fascinating company and good copy, and I cut short my London stay and took the *Golden Arrow* for the Continent. I went to the Hotel Scribe, his official headquarters, and found a note—but no Mr. Woods. He had sailed for America the day before. Later, in New York, he sent a case of champagne around to my hotel and an offer of $100 a week to play a small part, that of a reporter, in a play he was then producing. It was called *Hocus Pocus*. I then had no thought of returning to acting and suggested that he try to get Alexander Woollcott or Robert Benchley. "No!" screamed Al. "You're my man, sucker. Those fellows are professionals. They'd ruin my show. They'd also want too much money." He then made the pay $150 instead of $100 and I went into rehearsal and stayed with the company for two weeks or so. Just before the start of the dress rehearsal the director came to me and said, "Al wants to see you up in the office." Trouble, I thought. I went quickly to the Eltinge lift, made the slow ascent, and was soon admitted to his inner office. There he sat, feet on the desk, cigar ashes on his shirt front, and staring at the ceiling.

"Hello, sweetheart," he said. "Come in and sit down. . . . Now I've been watching you rehearse for a couple of weeks. If we were going to send this show on the road, where you wouldn't know anybody, it wouldn't be so bad. But I'm bringing it into New York and I just don't think you'd want to give that performance I've been seeing before a lot of your friends. I think it will be a good idea, sucker, if we just forget I tried to make an actor out of you. What's more, I'm going to cut your part right out of the play. Here . . . blow yourself to a week end in Atlantic City."

The envelope Al Woods gave me contained four weeks' salary.

*Hocus Pocus* never got to Broadway. It closed in the Bronx.

## *chapter nine*

~~~~~~~~~~

"BOY, get out and see things; the world's a big place," were the words of counsel to me from the shaggy-haired Charles Richmond, my Shakespearean reader friend, and I remembered them. When I joined the staff of *The New York Sun* I found myself working for the extraordinarily human Keats Speed, who believed in encouraging the individuality of all of his staff members and liked to go along with them as far as possible on all reasonable requests. He quite approved of the writing of my column from the far places in the theatrical off-season, feeling that copy from Utah or Nome or Cairo or La Paz would be more readable than summer-theater jottings, or reiterations of the fact that Broadway, in mid-summer, is the world's dullest place. I had begun a daily column in *The Sun* in the fall of 1926; I continued it, along with eight years of play reviewing, until tragedy struck at 280 Broadway on the morning of January 4, 1950.

During twenty-odd rich and crowded years with *The New York Sun* I thought up and worked out many of my own travel assignments; others came to me from Keats Speed or from the

city desk, with his approval. Once a city desk becomes convinced that it has a staff member who is always ready to "go
anywhere at once," as the rep-tent-and-tab performers used
to say in their at-liberty advertisements in *Billboard* (and perhaps they still do), the name of that reporter is likely to come
instantly to mind when some assignment, involving more or
less immediate departure, turns up. There was the time
when Mr. Speed (he was always "Mr." to everybody at the
plant except a few presumptuous and high-powered executives
on the business side) summoned me to his desk and, with his
slow smile, said, "We were wondering if you would feel like
flying to South America tomorrow afternoon." On another
occasion City Editor Bartnett asked me to meet him in the
library. I did so and he told me to prepare myself to fly all the
way across the Pacific, to Hong Kong and back, via Australia.
And in the wartime summer of 1942, Keats Speed, while
smoking his 11 A.M. cigarette as he walked up and down in the
corridor, sentrylike, and never going a step beyond his thirty-
foot course, said ever so quietly, "Mr. Morehouse, why don't
you go across the street to Rogers Peet and see if their tailor
could find a way of getting you into a correspondent's uniform?
We believe you'd get some good copy from our boys in the
British Isles. Perhaps the Army will put you aboard a troopship,
one of the big ones. There'd be a great story in the Atlantic
crossing."

I said, "Yes, sir. I'd like to write it." Two weeks later, fully
accredited by the War Department and looking fairly grotesque
in a uniform that had been shortened and widened and
chopped and sliced and slit and sewn, I reported that I was

sailing within twenty-four hours from a New York port with a mighty consignment of ready-for-combat infantrymen. "Fine," said Mr. Speed. "Go downstairs and get Mr. Luxton to give you some money. You won't need much; you're in the Army now."

That evening, braving the startled glances that my uniform, with its white "C" against a green background, brought on, I visited a few night spots, including the Stork Club, Twenty-One, and El Morocco. It was at Twenty-One, that world crossroads, that I was told, in a series of whispers that were fairly detonating, that my troopship was to be the *Queen Mary*, already loading at her North River pier; that I was to accompany 16,000 men of the renowned First Division, and right over in a corner, sitting there behind a highball, was the division's commanding officer—the lithe, wiry, colorful, outspoken, and mildly deaf Terry Allen, holding the rank of major general. I was presented to General Allen by the late Jack Kriendler, debonair saloonkeeper and perfectionist, a man of decision, humor, gaiety, and gallantry, who trained like a professional boxer for the job of running the bar floor at the dinner hour and the routine of exchanging greetings with some of the great of the world. General Allen glared at me and said, "How are you, Ward? . . . Don't call me General. My name is Terry. Glad to have you aboard. You can have the run of the ship." He kept his word, too.

I boarded the *Queen Mary*, hulking in the semiblackout at its well-guarded pier, around 11 P.M. the next night, bringing along a sixty-pound bag and two portable typewriters, it having been my experience that one machine generally breaks down, and that a typewriter mechanic is as difficult to find at a needed moment as an automobile mechanic or a steeplejack. There's also the fact that I have never put on a ribbon in all my city-room years. In travel, the only bellboy I ever found who could do the trick was a Filipino working for the Hotel Plains in Cheyenne.

Anyway, when the *Queen Mary* swung out into the sparkling sunlight of the Hudson at noon the next day, helped along by fussy tugs, and moved slowly toward the upper bay and then toward the Narrows, she was jammed—from top to bottom and bow to stern, with bunks everywhere except in the funnels—jammed with boys from the tobacco belt of Carolina and the plains of Kansas, from the mesa regions of New Mexico, the highlands of Virginia, and the green corners of Vermont. A lean, army-toughened private from one of the clock towns of Connecticut was at his post on the submarine watch; a burly, thickset sergeant, who used to run the Ferris wheel for an itinerant Middle West carnival, was alerted by his antiaircraft gun; a gigantic corporal, the one-time short-order cook for a lunch counter at Niagara Falls, stood ready with the gun crew of one of the big ones. Hard as rocks, these thousands of young Americans, who had learned the war games on the varied terrain of the nation's training areas—the rolling country, the piney woods, the sand hills, the sage and mesquite, the treeless ground, as flat as the floor. Now, with a life preserver worn every minute in every day and aboard an overladen warbound craft, they were watching and eating and sleeping and wondering, griping and laughing and talking and singing, reading and gazing and crouching on the decks, huddled together like quail in the broom sage, and pleading to the rolling dice.

During that crossing I shared narrow quarters with a Boston-born captain of infantry, who was later torn to bits by machine-gun fire. I talked with boys from the cedared hills of Oklahoma, the red-clay villages of Georgia, and the congested streets of Brooklyn. I sat down twice daily to beef, beans, boiled potatoes, and apricots and I looked in on more crap games than there were in the entire state of Nevada. I saw more lieutenants than I'd thought were alive, mislaid my life preserver twice, drank more coffee than I ever had in any year in my life, learned to tie a neat nautical bow, learned to climb into the upper bunk of a double-decker without spraining an ankle or breaking a leg, and became familiar with all the latest and most fascinating designs in tattoos—girls, birds, snakes, animals, flags, anchors. An infantryman from Sioux City, an erstwhile grocery clerk, won the sweepstakes: his girl's face done in red and blue, with her telephone number, was tattooed across his chest.

No shots were fired, no enemy was seen as the *Queen Mary*, a floating fortress, zigzagged across the blue-green Atlantic; no destination was announced, but rumors, rumors, rumors went the length of the ship. . . . "We're off Greenland." . . . "We're not far from the Azores." . . . "We're heading for Gibraltar." . . . "We're getting to Southampton." . . . "We're going to Africa." . . . "At least," observed Corporal Harpin of Jewett City, Connecticut, member of a gun crew, "we haven't turned around and we're not going back. We know that much."

Finally, after five days of tension, the great liner came to anchor just before daybreak in the Firth of Clyde off the Scottish coast. There was a rap at the door of Cabin M-37 and there stood a corporal I'd come to know, the Oregon lumberjack who was called the Golden Arm Kid; he had been tossing sevens and elevens, rattling the dice against an orange crate, ever since the *Queen* reached the open sea. "The General wants to see you, sir," said the corporal. "Right away."

I joined Terry Allen and General Theodore Roosevelt on the lighter for the trip to the shore in the uncertain half-light of that August morning of 1942. General Allen said, "We made that one. Now we'll see." And he was silent for the rest of the way. But Teddy Roosevelt jabbered on with the excitement of a well-read schoolboy coming upon the British Isles for the first time, mentioning this and that in Scottish history, talking of his eagerness to see England again, of the fitness of these 16,000 American boys who had been brought over for the great adventure—the invasion of the Continent.

The First Division was taken, via slow-moving troop-trains, to the south-central plain of England, near Salisbury. There, for some days, I was quartered in the house that had been assigned to Terry Allen, and I got to know him better. He was a good horseman and had been a crack polo player with the Seventh Cavalry; he was an excellent pistol shot and kept himself fit by calisthenics and two-mile jogs every afternoon; he talked fascinatingly of his boyhood in the Southwest and of the Mexican border country. I realized that his hearing, while impaired, was frequently good enough for him to hear what he wanted to hear, and I also realized that he was as eager to get to London as I was. I suggested the Hotel Savoy. He said fine, for me to go ahead and make the reservation. We'd leave on a Friday; he would have to be back on Monday. Good long week end.

So, early on Friday, the General's car, with a corporal at the wheel, spun to a stop at our doorway and we climbed in. "London, Jimmy," said the General to the boy from the Panhandle, out of Texas for the first time in his life. He merely said, "Yes, sir," and off he went. We saw England—the gabled houses, the quiet villages, the thatched cottages, the rolling fields, the camouflaged defenses in the valleys and over the uplands. On past the ivy-covered Jolly Farmer Inn, the King's Head Tavern, the Boar's Head Tavern, and the Fighting Cock, along roadways from which all direction markers had been removed, on past roadblocks and barbed-wire barricades, grim reminders of the invasion that England expected—and that never came.

Texas Jimmy, with a plainsman's instinct for direction, took few wrong turns; he was good at his map reading and seemed as familiar with left-side-of-the-road driving as if he'd been doing it all of his life. Terry Allen, as we rode along, kept up a running patter. . . . "Beautiful country, isn't it? I played polo here in 1921 and I was good, too. . . . Tea drinkers, these people. Never was much for tea in the States but over here they have the knack and the trick. The American soldier is a coffee drinker, and in the wardroom of a destroyer there's a fresh cup every ten minutes. Best cup of coffee I ever had in my life was at Eagle Pass, Texas, down on the border. Any cavalryman who has ever served at Eagle Pass will never forget it. . . . Great bunch we've brought over here. We've come for one purpose—to shoot and kill Nazi soldiers. We won't do that sitting around England; we know that. Sooner or later we'll be getting the hell out of here and heading across that channel. . . . Me? It will probably be a long time before I see the States again, if I ever do. My wife has $38,000 insurance and she'll be all right."

Texas Jimmy, with the unaccountable capacity for accomplishment that is peculiar to so many from his special playground in God's kingdom, found London. Unerringly through the outskirts and into the maze of the Strand and into the throbbing court of the plush Hotel Savoy. And there, during a bizarre week end, Terry Allen and I shared a royal suite. We entertained prodigally. Military friends came in to see the General; nonmilitary friends, all of the theater, were my visitors. Room-service waiters were forever bringing in trays and rolling in tables. . . . "You're fresh out of tonic water, sir," droned the floor captain. "Better 'ave a new supply, sir, and you'll soon be runnin' out of gin and Scotch too, sir."

There was a colonel in for dinner one evening and also a major, who had served, as a private, with the General in the St.-Mihiel offensive during World War I. There was a female star of the London stage in for lunch and a young dancer with hair of daffodil yellow and a young stage director and a celebrated actor who had played Iago in New York. Also, an American-born producer who had lived in England for years and also the dark-haired and vital young woman who played the Ophelia to John Barrymore's Hamlet. There was war talk, army talk, theater talk; telephone calls, telegrams, flowers, floor waiters. Into the tumult, right into the middle of it, came critic Richard Watts, calm, detached, informative, and just over from Dublin. He and the General fascinated each other for an hour. And then Watts, bored as hell, suggested that I join him in his room down the hall. We went along with gin-and-tonics, talked of the coming invasion (as all London would be doing for the next year) talked of the London theater and of the Irish theater, and of Terry Allen, praising him and damning him, and were engaged in giving the General something of a going-over when there came a sharp rap at the door. Watts went to it. There stood Terry Allen. He glared at us, smiled, and said, "Well, I understand you boys regard me as a great soldier, a goddam bore, and a deaf old bastard. . . . We'd all better get back to our place. One of your beautiful actress friends is on the way up."

When the revelry subsided, when the week end ended, when the Battle of the Savoy was fought and lost, and when the General decided that he would have to get on back to camp, and in a hurry, we called the cashier and asked that the bill be sent to the suite. In ten minutes or so up it came, via a page boy with a tray. We blinked as we looked it over—pounds, shillings, pence; precise, infinitesimal numerals in all the tiny spaces and squares. It all seemed so much Arabic but down in the corner was the total in pounds which, when translated, came to something around $466.

The General's shock was obviously greater than mine. As he wrote out his part of the check his only comment, and a quiet one, was "Hell, Ward, I never thought it would be this

high. We people in the Army can't live like you corre-
spondents!"

I went to Dover in September of 1942 and spent hours in
a fire-command post, just 21 miles from Cape Gris-Nez, the
French shore line—and the Germans. Heat haze shrouded the
channel, glassy in its stillness. Gulls looped about Shakespeare
Cliff, projecting itself sheerly above the pebbled beach. An
officer of the Royal Artillery was my guide. He talked articu-
lately, and in this fashion:
"If the visibility were a little better you could use glasses and
see the clock in the tower at Calais. That's how close we are
to Jerry. I've been here many months and have seen plenty.
Jerry has thrown a lot of bricks at us; it's on moonlight nights
that he likes to do his tricks. I wish I could put on a spot of
shooting for you. It would be jolly exciting, all right. . . .
Right here we have a ringside seat at the war. This town of
Dover has been through a lot—more than two thousand air-
raid warnings so far. An amazing garrison town. The defense
area along here is simply lousy with guns, like raisins in a cake,
and there's enough barbed wire along the beaches to reach
around the world and back. Thousands of people have been
evacuated from Dover—children, women, and old people—
but many of them have come back, and they go about their
daily lives just as if they might be living in Iowa. A fellow I
know had a garden in his back yard. Jerry came along and
threw a brick and blew a hole big enough to bury an army
truck. My gardening friend didn't seem to mind very much.

161

He's now got flowers growing on the bottom of the crater and around the sides. Sunken garden, he calls it. The only one in town. Other people use their craters for the kids to play in."

We left the fire command post and went to the quarters of my Royal Artillery officer. He bade me stand beside a window with a channel view as he ordered pink gins. Dover's air-raid siren began screaming.

"Hmm-m," he said, "sounds like she has a bad cold. That's the fifth this morning. . . . Dover's air raid shelters are under 240 feet of rock—really extraordinary. All the bombs in the world would never get under that chalk rock. Almost enough beds to take care of the entire population. Dover had around 40,000 people in 1939 but now, owing to evacuation, it's down to about 17,000. Got food under those cliffs to feed everybody for three months in case of an invasion. Lots of funny things keep happening. During the Battle of Britain a woman in Dover was taking a bath when a bomb or a shell or a land mine went off. It smashed her house to pieces. It crashed on down and there she was, sitting in the tub, and not hurt at all. Had hardly a stitch on when they got her over to the cliffs."

Dover's siren was moaning away, Jerry was somewhere overhead, and bombs were falling upon the north downs as my 5:45 train pulled hastily out of the station, London-bound.

The Army had brought me to the British Isles on that 1942 assignment; the Navy was taking me back, and I was directed to proceed to Belfast, Ireland, and on to Londonderry. Two weeks spent in Northern Ireland, with its heathered plains and soaring hills, rocky hummocks, and calm, silken rivers, two-wheeled carts and whitewashed houses, melancholy sheep and tea-drinking blacksmiths, convinced me that the people of Ulster had moved away en masse and that the sailors, soldiers, and marines of the United States had taken over—and to stay. The O'Donnells and the O'Neills and the McDevitts were nowhere in sight, but in their place I found the Joneses from Des Moines, the Smiths from Scranton, the Kaminskys from Brooklyn, and the Schultzes from Milwaukee.

Throughout all of that Irish north country wandered the inquisitive and warbound young men from the States. They banged about the old castles, marveled at the ancient Norman forts, muttered about the "Irish sunshine," had their drinks at the friendly pubs, rode in the jaunting carts, strolled in the forests of beech, holly, oak, ash, fir, and spruce, and were generally aware of the incredible beauty of the little glens, the stark headlands, and the mists over the Antrim hills.

I boarded a destroyer in the Firth of Foyle and made the voyage to New York. Three years later, as Germany surrendered, I was again sent to England in the outfit of a war correspondent, and was taken by Lieut. Comdr. Richard Aldrich, the Navy's public relations chief in the British Isles, for an air tour of sections of Germany. We stayed for several days in Bremen, a great city on the winding Weser, which had been ripped and battered and knocked flat by allied bombing in 174 raids. A mangled and shattered city, it offered mute and hideous testimony of the completeness of the German defeat. Half a church steeple in the center of town tilted grotesquely. A lone chimney reared itself from a square mile of obliterated masonry. Façades of a few stores remained pathetically vertical; close inspection revealed that their interiors were blackened and demolished. The opera house was gone, the carbarn smashed, and the hands of a big clock still standing in the wreckage of a big hotel revealed that the end came at 9:25.

When we returned to London, Commander Aldrich suggested a week's tour of southern England in a Navy car and with an American naval officer at the wheel. I wasn't quite sure of the name of the driver when we started on a westward course from London—Commander Aldrich merely called him Junkie—but I quickly realized that the left-hand rule had no terrors for him, that he had a passion for cathedrals, and that he frequently suggested stops in little and big towns to visit the cathedrals and the antique shops. By the time we got to Bath he seemed to have bought at least two thousand dollars' worth of antiques, and I remarked to the Commander that it was a little surprising to find a navy chauffeur with such an appreciation of old brass and porcelain, bits of china and silver, odd pieces of furniture, and that our man seemed to have quite a lot of money to throw around. Oh, yes, said Commander Aldrich. Oh, yes, indeed. Perhaps I didn't realize just who the driver was. Then he effected a formal introduction—Mr. M., meet Mr. Julius Fleischmann, a gentleman with financial interest in yeast, gin, the ballet, real estate, oil, copper, gold, and Bolivian tin. Mr. Fleischmann indeed—world traveler, yachtsman, homeowner in Cincinnati and Cape Cod, ballet lover, and host extraordinary, who was even then thinking that if he had to live in New York he would want a view of the park and that a fairly sure way of getting it was to own a hotel along Fifth Avenue. "Remind me," Junkie said to Aldrich as we paused for lunch at Torquay, "to buy the Sherry-Netherland when I get back to New York."

When I sailed from England on this trip in 1945 it was aboard the *Queen Elizabeth,* which, like the *Mary,* had been heroically engaged in the ferrying of troops back and forth across the Atlantic. I got aboard the *Elizabeth* in the Firth of Clyde. For half a day, before sailing, I was without a bunk. The sergeant who seemed to have a lot to say in the matter of the room assignments came to me as I was sitting on the floor in a corridor. "You're the New York dramatic critic, aren't you?" he asked. Yeah, I said. Well, he said, he lived in Chicago and he'd done a little acting and he was interested in the theater, and perhaps some time I could give him some letters to the big managers? Could I! I couldn't produce Belasco or Charles Frohman, but if he'd like to meet Aldrich & Myers and Josh Logan and Kermit Bloomgarden, it might be arranged. If Jed Harris wouldn't scare hell out of him he could meet him, too. And perhaps he'd enjoy going to lunch with Gilbert Miller and dining with Lee Shubert? Hell, anything. I needed a place in which to write; I had six or seven pieces to finish on the return crossing; I didn't feel that I could do such a job in the room with fourteen colonels, from which I had fled to the corridor. "Come with me," said the sergeant. He led the way to another deck and to an enormous outside stateroom with private bath and two portholes. Then he said, "This is yours. Keep the door locked and don't let anybody see it. I think you'll be comfortable."

The sergeant got those Broadway letters.

## *chapter ten*

~~~~~~~~~~~~~~

EVER since I wore knee pants, ever since the days when I was doing my swimming in Olympia's Blue Sink and in the black water beneath the railroad trestle just out of Guyton, Georgia, I've had a passion for getting around, and for plays enacted by living actors. I've liked travel; I've liked the theater—good, bad, and terrible. The theater and travel. Take up both early in life and they stay with you. Those who must have their theater will somehow find it; those with that craving to see what's beyond the next hill will somehow see it. I once picked cotton all day in the burning south-Georgia sun for the money to see a road company in *Graustark*; I once sold my bicycle to get the fare to the middle-Georgia city of Macon. Didn't know a soul there, had no reason for going except that I just wanted to see what Macon was like.

I never cared for organized sightseeing and was never one for a regimented junket, such as those that are so frequently offered to newspapermen, but in more or less lone-wolf fashion I've been about. Such places as Tierra del Fuego and Pine Bluff, Arkansas, have thus far eluded me, but I've known the excitement of the two-mile-high city of La Paz, have walked along main street in Nome, heard the surf pounding against the rocks of Biarritz, descended deep into the gold mines of the Transvaal around Johannesburg, and have enjoyed the beauty of the azaleas of Natchez, the hydrangeas of Thomasville, Georgia, and the tall pines of Oregon. I've somehow denied myself the Grand Canyon. It will wait for me. I feel that if you have the travel urge at nine you will also have it at ninety.

I definitely find myself stirred, and often, by thoughts of extensive wanderings. There are impressions that stay vividly alive: the glistening mosques and minarets of Istanbul, sprawled spectacularly beside the Golden Horn; the magnificent hump of Pikes Peak as first seen in the northward drive into Colorado from New Mexico; the bench-sitters in the sparkling spring sunshine along the Champs Elysees; the clouds of pink flamingos that come into view in flying along the eastern margins of Latin America. I once saw a Polynesian boy eat a raw fish on Canton Island, that tiny strip of coral in the mid-Pacific; I was startled when Mount Saint Helens, looking like a great snowball, rose suddenly from the plain in the American northwest, and I've had the feeling of great peace as I've strolled about Stratford-on-Avon, the town of Shakespeare's birth, with its gabled houses, its little shops, its quiet streets—a town so thoroughly representative of Britain's timelessness and restfulness, its intellectuality, spirituality, and solidity.

Travel, once you've had it, is yours. Travel and its impressions, the theater and the impact of it, can never be taken from you. A man who insists upon moving about, whether by plane or train, by boat or motorcar, is certain to experience some torturing hours, some dismal journeys. A man who goes in for the theater every chance he gets, who would rather go to a play than to a movie or to an opera or to hear a symphony orchestra or sit home with a television set, is certain to come upon drama that is tormentingly dull, upon plays that are atrociously acted. But the bad plays are quickly forgotten; the good plays stay with you. Magnificent acting is unforgettable; so are many of the theater's great moments. I can still hear the wail of Sadie Thompson's phonograph in *Rain* as if she just turned it on last night. I shall always cherish the memory of the haggard and filthy, but heroic, Captain Flagg quitting the pleasures of Cognac Pete's for the journey back to the front lines. Certainly Katharine Cornell left an impression that is lasting with her touching performance as the daugher in *A Bill of Divorcement*. So did Dudley Digges with his boozy old saloonkeeper in *The Iceman Cometh*, Emily Stevens with her electric playing of a desperate and unhappy woman in *Hedda Gabler*, Alfred Lunt with his bounce and unpredictability in Tarkington's *Clarence*, Lynn Fontanne with her mastery of character in *Elizabeth the Queen*, Richard B. Harrison with the majesty and grandeur that he brought to the role of De Lawd in *The Green Pastures*, William Gillette with the expertness of his underplaying in *Sherlock Holmes*. And George M. Cohan, with the lesson in acting that he gave all members of his profession in his own melodrama, *Gambling*.

The theater and travel. Sound investments they were for

me in tender years. The performance of a road actor, Geoffrey C. Stein, in a second company of Clyde Fitch's *The City*, remains as vivid as that of Barrymore in *Hamlet*. The chant of the fishermen pulling in their nets at Alexandria seems to have been heard only last night, and it must have been only yesterday that I sipped the Turkish coffee and brandy as served by an amiable Arab on the shore of the Dead Sea. I shall always remember the excitement of the chariot race in *Ben Hur*, the charm and the romance of *Merely Mary Ann*. I doubt if I'll forget the picturesqueness of Green River, Wyoming, or the red, red roofs of Auckland, New Zealand, or the terror of the inhabitants of Cairo, Illinois, walled in by sandbags at flood time along the Mississippi.

Yes, in travel you *do* meet people. . . . The poet-playwright, Christopher Fry, a shy, gentle, and gracious man, talked with me in Oxford of his love for England and of its being a land in which "things have happened." Jan Christian Smuts, the great man of the Union of South Africa, spoke gravely of his belief that a third World War is inevitable as he received me in Pretoria. And there was Michael Arlen at a bar in Athens, sipping ouze, and chattering away gaily of his appreciation of the good looks of American women.

"I love this town," said Katharine Hepburn, as she sprawled in her slacks before an open fire at Claridge's in London. "Love it, adore it, but I can't get used to being here; I feel like I've been hit over the head." . . . "Out here," said Ina Claire, as she gazed upon the beauty of San Francisco from her Nob Hill apartment, "I do nothing. I just sit. I sit and look. I'm just so happy I'm sort of suspended." . . . "Vivian and I love playing

New York," murmured Laurence Olivier in his duplex apartment in London's Christ Church Street, "but I still remember that during the Old Vic engagement the $400 a week they gave me wasn't enough to pay our bill at the St. Regis."

Quotes can be very vital when they are accurately recorded. It's always been important to me to put down the words, in an interview, just as they were spoken. . . . Such words as those of . . . Katharine Cornell (in Cleveland), "I've never been without stage fright in my life, but I'm able to control it better now than I was in youthful years." . . . Irving Berlin (in Paris), "Some day I want to do my dream revue at the Music Box—a three-period revue, containing all the old song hits through the years." . . . Anita Loos (in Philadelphia), "My mother was a refined woman and my father was a charming tramp." . . . Lillian Hellman (in Baltimore), "I'm lazy. I dawdle in getting to work. I suppose I talk so much about research because I like to stall." . . . Ty Cobb (in Twin Falls, Idaho), "I never intentionally tried to spike but two men in my life. One of them was Dutch Leonard, the pitcher, and the other Lou Criger, the catcher." . . . Raymond Massey (in Boston), "John Drew got me started in the theater. He said, 'My boy, go to London and go on the stage. You'll get a job as an American actor.' I did." . . . Elia Kazan (in London), "The American theater is the greatest in the world, but what a place London is for trying out plays! You can do one for four thousand dollars. We have something priceless in America—playwrights who write plays about America." . . . Cole Porter (in Boston), "I like people. I like the human race. It has become fashionable to be nice to people

in the theater—especially to the kids who're just starting." . . .
And there was Emlyn Williams, the actor-author-director, talking in London, "I've always been just going to play Hamlet, and I really want to do it in the end. I'd love to try it with a good director."


I've made the complete around-the-world trip via the airways, doing it in three and a half weeks and touching ground only thirteen times. Such a trip can be completed in half of the time of my global spin, or even less, but if I ever try it again I shall insist upon six weeks or even six months.

My course was eastward all the way after making the run from New York to Gander, up there in the Newfoundland wilderness—eastward to Paris and on to Rome and to Beirut, capital of that little sliver of a Mediterranean-front country called Lebanon. Then on to Karachi, new state of Pakistan, via Basra, and on to Calcutta. I skipped Rangoon and Burma but stayed for five days in Bangkok, Thailand. Hong Kong was next on my course. Then there was a northward detour to Tokyo, and from Tokyo I flew on to Wake Island, to Hawaii, to San Francisco, and back to New York. Such flying, inclusive of a side trip to the north-India hill station called Darjeeling, gives you a total of some 23,000 miles, and in doing it you have soared above bays, straits, seas, and a couple of oceans. It was too fast, I decided once the wheels of my San Francisco-to-New York plane had touched ground at La Guardia Airport, but even in such whirlwind travel there are things that leave an imprint upon your memory. . . .

The pastel roofs of Paris as your Pan American World Airways Clipper circles for a landing in the approach to Orly Field; the noontime Parisian traffic whipping dizzily around the Place Etoile and somehow uncoiling after getting into nightmarish tangles; the hilly, jangling, Arabic-speaking port of Beirut, jutting out into the sea; the great immensity of earth en route to Karachi, as bright as glass under the burning heat of a summer's sun; the beauty, the squalor, the heat, the color of the overpopulated city of Calcutta; the airport on the Kowloon Peninsula, lying beyond the Red-held islands, at tumultuous Hong Kong, and the snowy cone of Fujiyama, thrusting itself through the clouds and visible from your plane cabin as you streak through the sky toward Tokyo. There were pages and pages of notebook jottings in support of such impressions and there were more pages, many more, on my trip to Darjeeling. Perhaps I'll never live to climb Mount Everest; I may never even see it, but I intend to try, and to do so another visit to Darjeeling will be necessary.

When you return from an around-the-world jaunt there is an even chance that someone will say, "Now, of all the places that you visited, what spot did you like best? What place left the greatest impression?" Several persons spoke to me in that fashion and they appeared to be listening as I gave the quick reply, "Darjeeling," and then tried to say why. Darjeeling is an extraordinary town, scattered over the hills near the Nepal border, a town that slants this way and that, and that offers, on a good day, a magnificent view of the great Himalayan panorama, with Kanchenjunga rising to a mere 28,146 feet. It's topped by Mount Everest and its 29,002 feet.

If you're in Calcutta, as I was, and want that trip to Darjeeling, and are willing to put in a lot of time and money on the chance of seeing Everest, the world's highest mountain, you leave Calcutta's teeming Chowringhee Road around 6 A.M., report at the offices of Airways India, Inc., and you're taken through the oven-hot, cattle-filled, humanity-packed streets on a wheezy bus to Dum-Dum Airport. Then, in an hour or so, you're aboard a twin-motored plane, which seems feather-light in comparison with the four-motored Pan American Clippers, and after a great deal of bouncing around and a flight of about 300 miles, you're set down at the Bagdogra Airport at the end of the line. It's then that the perils really begin.

My round-trip ticket from Calcutta to Darjeeling was inclusive of automobile transportation from Bagdogra over fifty-seven miles of winding roadway to the Himalayan town, a trip that isn't done in less than three hours. The three seemed like seven and the fifty-seven miles like one hundred and seventy. There are more sharp turns in the highway than you'll find in all of the Great Smoky Mountains; your driver blows his horn more or less continuously, and you are forever meeting jaunty little trains which use the narrow-gauge mountain railway, and which are often tearing along beside your car or whirling around the turns. And it's generally on one of the hairpin curves, as yellow dust scutters across the roadway, that another car or truck appears just ahead, and without bothering to stay on its own side of the road. My driver on the Bagdogra-to-Darjeeling haul was a fellow accustomed to such emergencies and a man of instantaneous reflexes. He'd merely give his wheel a slight jerk and he would generally laugh as we got through.

Once in Darjeeling, after a fifteen-minute pause in the 4864-foot-high town of Kurseong, which seemed so hospitable, so immovable, so protectingly anchored, I went immediately to the big and rambling Mount Everest Hotel, talked with the gracious Viennese woman who runs it, and sat down to the finest meal I'd had since Paris. I spent the afternoon enjoying the out-of-season solitude of Mrs. Kruschandl's inn, retired early, and was awakened at 3:30 A.M. by my room-bearer, bringing along a breakfast tray of eggs and chicken livers, juice and coffee. He returned within a few minutes to tell me that it had been raining all night and that the car that was to take me to Tiger Hill had arrived. If you're to see Mount Everest you go first to Tiger Hill.

I got into the car and found that I'd drawn a fellow adventurer, one Mr. Suresh Chandra, an optician from Calcutta, who was carrying a small red-and-blue umbrella and wearing the familiar Hindu dhoti. The fog-shrouded road was wet and winding; our car crept along for almost an hour, going steadily uphill, and it finally stopped with a jerk. "Now," our man said, "that's all. Now you walk. Car can't go up. I wait here for you."

Mr. Chandra and I got to the crest of Tiger Hill after a great deal of climbing and puffing and for two shivering hours, just before the break of day, waited in the mist and fog. It was a vigil that promised a glimpse of the icy tip of the tallest thing upon this earth. But no luck. There was no sunrise. The fog became thicker, the Himalayan air grew colder. I suggested an ascent of the stairway that led to the top of Tiger Hill's cement observation tower. But Suresh Chandra, with the acute reasoning of the East, said, "Why? It is only more up."

Finally, at 7 A.M. after waiting like duck shooters for the birds to come into the decoys, we gave up and took the slippery downhill trail to the waiting car. . . . Tiger Hill hasn't seen the last of me. Mount Everest isn't going anywhere, and there will come a morning when I'll be there again and the sun will be up and the mountain out.

Yes, it was Darjeeling, and the trip to it, that left me with strongest impressions from my around-the-world flight. And there was also Bangkok, Asiatic and irresistible, lying beside the muddy river called the Chao Phraya and not far from the Gulf of Siam, and often the place that is the main objective of people who have the time, and can find the money, for a globe-circling adventure. The vivid and kaleidoscopic Bangkok is a town as flat as the floor—three feet above sea level. It's a place of a myriad sights, sounds, and incantations—a city of gilded spires, bejeweled temples, blue-and-gold tiled roofs, glaring, leering demons in mosaic and stone, and such architectural whimsies as overlapping roofs and upcurling, serpentlike effects at the gables.

Sure, there are canals (or klongs) all over the place, and yellow-robed Buddhist priests and three-wheeled bicycle rickshas called samlohs, and there are Siamese, unnumbered thousands of Chinese, and about 1100 Americans, but don't go there expecting to find elephants pushing teak logs around on New Road. All of that belongs to the upcountry and to the Siam that used to be. There are probably a million or two young Siamese who have never even seen an elephant, but they've seen Buicks and Fords and Cadillacs and DeSotos—leave anybody out? And—oh, yes—Jaguars. Seems that His Royal Highness, King Plumiphon Aduldet, has a Jaguar and drives it like hell.

It's in Bangkok (population around a million)—strange, mystic, congested, fascinating—that you are given the impression that everybody is busy. They're not hungry and they're working at something or other. There are customers in the shops, in the sidewalk stalls; people besides the resident and visiting Americans are spending their ticals. A woman selling post cards in the Temple of the Reclining Buddha easily made change for a 100-baht note ($5); a girl with a cold-drink cart on New Road had a queue of four patrons as I paused with ticals in hand; the restaurant called Chez Eve, the only air-cooled eating place in town, was jammed at lunch, and I was told that Hoi Thien Lau would be that way when I went for a Chinese dinner.

There were Americans in Bangkok who cursed the heat—it was 102 degrees at the time of my arrival—but, with something of defiance, they insisted that it is actually no hotter than St. Louis or Fort Worth or New York in mid-July, and they would generally go on to tell me about the advantages that life in Thailand offered.

"Take my setup," said a member of the American colony as we ordered luncheon—spinach soup, club sandwich, and the root-vegetable dessert *gula malacca*, served with coconut cream and sirup—at the Chez Eve. "I have a nice house and eight servants. They're highly specialized. There is the number-one boy, who is a girl, and we have a cook, a coolie for the cleaning, a gardener, a guard for the house at night, a nurse for our two kids, a driver, and the fellow who does the laundry. Eight servants—they're willing and efficient and charming—and we get it all for $115 a month!"

That American's words found their way into my notebook, as did those of a Bangkok businessman, one L. G. Harrison, who observed, "We've been trying to sell tractors to the people of Thailand, but it seems that it will be a long time before they're ready for American machinery. The truth is, the government doesn't want the country mechanized. The Thai farmer has his water buffalo and he is generally a happy man. He considers himself a rich one. His land is fertile, he raises all the food he needs, he's never cold, and he doesn't have to bother about clothes."

And there was the informal, flavorful speech of other far-from-home Americans that you record as it is spoken, and that stays in your memory. . . . "Life out this way," said Patrick J. Sullivan, Jr., in Karachi, Pakistan, "can be very rugged for American wives, but it's a life with many enjoyments. We don't live by the clock as you do back home; there's nothing here that's *got* to be done in the next five minutes." . . . "Calcutta," said R. K. Spurr, an English journalist, as he talked with me in that overloaded metropolis, "is a sad and desolate city, a tragic city, a city dying on its feet. Those thousands upon thousands of Bengalis sleep in the street because they have no other place to go." . . . "That play called *The King and I,*" said Jimmie Thompson of the Thai Silk Company, as we dined at Bangkok's Hotel Oriental, "is the best advertisement Siam ever had. I've had dozens of Americans tell me it's the thing that made them want to see Bangkok." And there were these words from Carl Dorris of Denver, out there in Basra, Iraq, south of the Garden of Eden country, as sales manager for the Pan American World Airways, "This Basra is a hell of a place. If you like dates, and are sure you will never get tired of dates, you should get your wife and come here and just settle along the Shatt-Al-Arab River. It's the country that gives the world about eighty per cent of its date supply. If you like dates you should have been around my house for the past year. We've had date pie, date custard, date cookies, date ice cream, date everything. But don't mention the word to my wife if you do come to see us. She'll scream."

It's entirely possible, notwithstanding visits to such places as Darjeeling and Bangkok, La Paz and Buenos Aires, Leopoldville and Johannesburg since leaving the city room of the *Atlanta Journal,* that the travel I've enjoyed most has been found in wandering about the United States of America in a vehicle propelled by gasoline. If you go from coast to coast by stratocruiser you see beautiful layers of clouds—and little else. From a window of the rocketing *Super Chief* the blurred landscape flits past. From an automobile, and with an automobile, you see America close up. It's all there for you, with superhighways, nonsuperhighways, good roads, and bad roads, cleaving the states like so many tentacles, crisscrossing their way into the remote areas, twisting around the sheer sides of mountains, burrowing under hills, uncoiling through the valleys and across the uplands.

I've found great excitement in going into the nooks and

corners of America, in turning into the little roads that branch off from the main highway and wind off into the hills. I've liked the sights and the revelations of the great American roadside, the little touches here and there of our everyday life: a gnarled old gentleman on his front porch in Holbrook, Arizona, just sitting there quietly and watching the passing parade; a girl in a smoke-blue sweater, driving a truck in Peru, Indiana, and lighting a cigarette as the traffic light turns to red; a woman in Iowa, back home with treasures from the supermarket, pausing to lift the latch on her front grate.

In this America of ours, as of 1953, the motor court has become a national mania; it represents a trend and a craze. If the great Sarah Bernhardt were trouping the continent today, with one leg or two, she would probably be playing under canvas, as in the old days, but she would be staying in the motels. They have become a part of the true Americana, along with those supermarkets and the drive-in theaters, the coffee shops and the juke boxes, the trailer camps and the detour signs.

From the ringside seat that motorcar travel affords you see your countrymen as they sweep their porches and water their lawns, walk in the parks and jaywalk at the intersections, fish from the highway bridges, double-park on Main Street, and dawdle at the drugstore fountains. In this high-pressure land of ours, the old-fashioned trolley car still rattles into sight here and there, stubbornly in survival; the old-fashioned locomotive is still grinding along, smokily and explosively, on many stretches of track; barbershops are still called the Elite, and drugstores, blindingly lighted, have become so modernized and overcluttered that the prescription counter has shrunken to a mere ledge, and an invisible one at that.

There are towns, little towns, that leave their impressions from across-America wanderings; cities, too. There's the river hamlet of Union, Nebraska, where the West seems to begin; there's Lyman, Wyoming, which suggests the ultimate in remoteness, and Jacksonville, Illinois, a college town, one of the prettiest in America, with great trees, wide lawns, attractive houses, and seemingly representative of America's repose, comfort, and stability. I like Kokomo, Indiana, chosen by Booth Tarkington and Harry Leon Wilson as the home town of their homespun lawyer, Daniel Vorhees Pike, principal character in their enduring play *The Man from Home*. I shall always remember Coalville, Utah, because a particularly pleasant woman running a lunch stand sold me a quart of hot coffee for a dime, but added, regretfully, that she would have to ask forty cents for the container, a fruit jar. I shall always be fascinated with Mark Twain's boyhood town of Hannibal, Missouri, snuggled beside the great Mississippi, and which manufactures shoes, stoves, buttons, cigars, cement; it's there that the picture theater is called the Tom Sawyer and the dinette bears the name of Twain. I'm among those under the spell of the beauty of San Francisco, a city built in tiers. The charm of Richmond-on-the-James remains unforgettable; Butte, Montana, city with the frontier touch, stays in my memory; there is always an urge to return to the glary and roaring town of Las Vegas, Nevada, hell-red with neons. I like the bustle of the town square in Mount Pleasant, Iowa, the drowsiness of the village (population 300), of Register, Georgia, which is near the fabulous general store of the 300-pound and oddly roguish Moses Jackson Bowen; it offers everything from side meat to sewing machines, millinery to fishhooks.

And then, of course, there's Pittsburgh. There's always Pittsburgh. A tilted city, a metropolis magnificently askew—a place of hills, gulches, steel, iron, slag, grime, heat, and cinders, with gruff stacks forever pouring forth an ocherous smoke. Pittsburgh, with beautiful homes and huddles of shacks, many of them buckled precariously to the hillsides; Pittsburgh with its roaring furnaces, sluggish rivers, and stark bridges strung across them, is inextinguishable; it stands as a symbol of America's might, its productivity and its potentialities.

Yes, in this land of ours, with the silvered watertanks visible through the haze ten miles away, fine highways streaking across the prairie and glinting in the sun, with its dust storms and hailstorms, mesas and mountain peaks, great elms and cottonwood trees, a man who wants to get into a car and wander about won't fret for lack of variety. America is hot and it's cold, it's sticky and it's frigid, it's flat and it's hilly, dry and wet, cloudy and glary. Also, it's big—and pretty wonderful. You could drive about for twenty years, going this way and that, and you'd never run out of roads. There'll always be things you will want to see; always that next town and something lying beyond that other hill. No interrogations at the state borders; no curtains, iron or otherwise, as you move about. A great immensity of earth. Bigger than you thought it would be, more exciting than you thought it could be.

I have frequently tried, in moments when I've been away

181

from the frenzy of New York, to go in for enough introspection to find out something about the kind of person I am, have been, and am getting to be, and to meditate upon what effect the impact of New York has had and is having. I've often wondered, in comparatively relaxed moments afforded by far-from-Broadway rovings, how I would have fared if I had accepted my father's offer to join him in the lumber business. Or if I'd really believed the lovely Julia Boyle when she told me I had a talent for painting. Or if I had turned to professional acting, or if I had stuck to playwrighting with the zest that I gave to it in teen-age years.

I've always regarded the typewriter as a good friend; I've never looked upon writing as a chore. Perhaps the wording and organization of a "lead," as the top paragraphs are called in the city room, has occasionally been irksome, but once that first few minutes is past I've actually found an acute satisfaction in sitting before a keyboard. I've enjoyed the isolation and the sense of insulation that this business of writing provides. It's always been my notion that a writer's surroundings should be as pleasant as possible, and I've sought to go in for comfort in the choice of a workroom—my favorite, the beautiful Ritz-Carlton in the city of Boston. The sea is out one window, as represented by the Charles River; the effect of the woods and the valleys is created by the park, just below the other window. The commissary is available via a pearl button in the wall; the slightest touch brings an instantaneous response from a genie with a food card. Plays and vital new scenes of plays are written at Boston's Ritz. Books and parts of books are written within its hospitable walls. I've done portions of five books in this magnificently operated hotel that stands at Arlington and Newbury; I shall again be clamoring for quarters on the top floor when I return to playwrighting.

In the process of finding out about myself—introspection comes easy when you're waiting, say, in Green River, Wyoming, for three days as the only available mechanic works on your car—I well know that I've never known a moment when I *had* to have company. When I have work to do, and I've never known the day when some hadn't piled up, I actually enjoy being alone. Depression is something that is infrequent with me and short-lived; I've always had something of a sublime optimism and something of an oh-well-the-rainy-days-will-take-care-of-themselves attitude and don't honestly believe that I've known a moment of envy in my life. It's always been my belief that God's blessings are spread around; if something good happens to a competitor, it can also happen to me; if great good fortune comes to some friend of mine, or to somebody I know, I've often had exactly this thought, "That's fine. My turn will be next."

Being one who is guided a great deal—undoubtedly too much—by impulses and emotions and first impressions, I've always felt that I knew, immediately upon meeting a person, whether I liked that person or didn't, and I've found that I've seldom had to reverse, or revise, the first instantaneous judgment. Like all of us, I've often deplored the self-centered ways of our fellow man, but have been heartened by the display of decency and generosity in human beings in an emergency. Or in any kind of catastrophe. Or in even the slightest of street accidents. Let a man slip and fall on the subway stairs in the supposedly cold-blooded and always-in-a-hell-of-a-rush New York and there will be two or three persons who will instantly forget the urgency of their own missions and go hastily to his assistance.

I've never actually thought a great deal about God or the possibilities, probabilities, and penalties of immortality. I don't believe I've ever experienced any actual uneasiness about old age, feeling that I'd somehow be immune to it, and knowing that I have had, and have now, a protective self-sufficiency. Give me the Ritz, or just a bare room with a typewriter, and I know that I can amuse myself; give me a pad and pencil and I know that I can sit contentedly for hours in a duckblind or beside a stump-filled pond that is filled, theoretically, with fish.

I'm a writer who likes to work in the mornings. If I'd been one of those given to all-night endurance drives my output would have been enormous. I've never gone in for night writing except for the back-at-the-office play reviews. When you're working for a morning paper as a dramatic critic you race to make the deadline; if you're an afternoon paper reviewer you still try to get your impressions and decisions upon paper with all possible speed. In the first place, it's your understanding with your office that the review will be put into type as fast as possible. And there is also the fact that a critic rushing home to bed right after a performance, with the resolve to rise at 5 A.M. and write his review, would suffer a night of torment, and probably get no sleep at all.

## chapter eleven

THERE is something terrifying in knowing that a great newspaper is slipping dangerously, something utterly shattering in being with one when death comes.

We all knew that *The New York Sun*, a distinguished daily for more than a century, was in a state of decline beginning with the spring of 1947, and just after it had reached a circulation mark that was practically the highest in its history. The falling-off began with the withdrawal of all the advertising of a big department store, this action being followed by the inexplicable and unaccountable disappearance of the business of two other great stores. Other accounts were lost—and *The Sun* was doomed. Negotiations between the management and Roy Howard, representing the Scripps-Howard interests, began in the early summer of 1949. The meetings went along with almost melodramatic secrecy, all those participating being pledged to silence. Rumors of the sale of *The Sun*, which had been spreading for all of two years, and which brought on frequent denials, continued and became wilder as the months went by. But the developments leading to the actual sale were guarded so carefully *The Sun's* city editor, Edmond Bartnett, whose duties were actually those of a managing editor and whose counsel had been frequently sought on matters of policy and operation, did not know the dreadful truth, didn't even suspect it, until he was told on the Friday before the Wednesday of the announcement. That Wednesday was January 4, 1950, the day that *The New York Sun* appeared for the last time.

Bartnett, like those of his staff, had been disturbed for many months by the recurrent rumors. He had known, of course, that the paper was losing money and that the sharp drop in revenue from advertising had been accompanied by a gradually diminishing circulation. He knew that such conditions could not go on indefinitely, but it was inconceivable to him that an institution like *The Sun,* one hundred and sixteen years old, could suddenly go out of business. He undoubtedly suspected, as most of us did, that it would be sold sooner or later, and he well knew that Thomas W. Dewart was weary of the task of keeping it going. But any thought of the paper's abrupt discontinuance, of its being killed off, had never come to his mind. He had expected, as did we all, that some new ownership would eventually take over and that there would be revitalization under a management with the heart, and the ability, to fight the forces that had marked the paper for destruction.

My telephone rang at eight-fifteen on the morning of January 4, 1950. I was up, but had not expected a call. Willie Priory, my loyal assistant for twenty years, was on the wire. He fairly screeched his words, "The paper's been sold! . . .

You don't have to do a column for tomorrow. No more paper after today." I broke into his screaming and asked, *"Who bought the paper?"* He told me and went on hysterically, "There's a panic down here. Everybody's crying. Nobody knows what the hell they're going to do. Better come on down here." I told him I'd be down in an hour.

*The Sun* was sold. I just sat there by the telephone, stunned and numbed. So there was some basis for all the rumors of the past two, three, and four years, rumors that actually started when the advertising was up, when the circulation was rising, when the paper was passing around $1000 bonus checks to department heads at Christmas. So a wealthy Broadway showman hadn't been quite so crazy, three years before, when he asked me to meet him uptown, told me that he was in the market to buy a good newspaper, and that he had heard from a Wall Street source that the Dewarts wanted to get out of the newspaper business and to waste no time about it.

*The Sun* was sold. There, in four words, was the desolating and crushing truth. Certain things of the past few months now took on a revealing significance, spinning through my head. I now realized why our fine executive editor, Keats Speed, loved by us all, had almost collapsed when he walked into a surprise party given for him by eighty-odd staff members on the evening of October 1, 1949. Tears flooded his eyes. During the hours that followed, as he sought to become a part of the merriment, he was fairly agonized by the knowledge that all these good friends were being sold out; that the money for the purchase hadn't been yet handed over but that *The Sun* was as good as out of business. During that evening he must have felt an urge to give them news that he thought they deserved to have, but he had taken that vow of secrecy. An evening that had been intended as one of tribute and triumph for him turned out to be the greatest ordeal of his life.

No wonder Keats Speed had said, "See me about it next week," when I went to him, on the afternoon of January 2, regarding some special coverage for an impending Broadway event. No wonder he had scribbled his initials on an expense account for a trip to Istanbul, completed just before Christmas, without his usual close scrutiny of the figures. No wonder he had seemed so haggard during the past six months as he made ever-increasing trips past the door of my corridor office to the elevators for the ascent to those seventh-floor conferences. No wonder he had been so subdued in his denials of rumors, in compliance with his promise, and had been so uncommunicative when members of the editorial department spoke to him of advertising, of circulation, and of the paper's prospects. No wonder, indeed, that he had aged so perceptibly within a half year. A man with a soul, Keats Speed, a man of decency and depth and great sensitivity and feeling of responsibility, and it had all been a torturing experience.

*The Sun* was sold. Once the great shock of it was over, the first thought of every staff man was this, "What do I do now?" Every man instantly realized that security, as represented by employment on a paper he loved, had suddenly vanished, and that a whole new career would have to be started elsewhere—and at once. In my own case, I was a dramatic critic when I went to bed the night before, and I now recalled Jed Harris's sardonic words in talking of critics and criticism, "A critic is a critic so long as he is on a paper; if he loses his job, or his paper folds, he is no longer a critic." The night before, I was on a payroll and earning good money. Now I was off a payroll and that hadn't happened for a day in my life since I'd gone to work as a cub in Savannah. What now, I thought, as I just sat there beside the telephone . . . sat there for a full fifteen minutes. Would I now call *The New York Times* or *Time* magazine. Or decide that this was the time to quit the tumult of New York and take up life in the great Southwest, somewhere around Socorro, New Mexico, or just pack up and return to Atlanta, a city I'd always loved.

I went into my wife's room and told her the news. After a half minute or so she said, and with a degree of excitement, "Why, darling, this will be an adventure!" I said, "Yeah, and a good one—I hope." I went back to my own telephone, and called Barclay 7-3211, and asked for B. O. McAnney, the managing editor of the *World-Telegram*, with whom I had worked upon coming up from Georgia and a man I had always liked and respected. "Bo," I said, "this is Ward Morehouse. Do you need a good rewrite man?" He laughed. "Don't go shopping around. We want you over here. . . . Sit there a few minutes. Lee Wood will call you." Within a half hour Lee Wood did call. Very affable, too. Could I come in to see him around twelve o'clock? Well, on the stroke of noon I arrived at 125 Barclay Street, opposite Pier 17, and took the elevator to the third floor. By twelve-ten I was working for Scripps-Howard. I then went downstairs and went back to the *Sun* building to spend the day.

The news of *The Sun's* passing had been given to members of the staff by a notice put on the bulletin board at exactly 8:04 A.M., January 4, sent over by City Editor Bartnett in accordance with instructions given him—the cold, brutal, abrupt announcement that *The Sun* was dead. The copy boy who took the notice across the room had read it on the way; within a minute or two there was a stampede to the board. A thunderbolt had struck on the second floor at 280 Broadway; the reactions of staff members were those of men stunned and flabbergasted, as had been the reaction of City Editor Bartnett when Keats Speed had called him in on Friday and told him that the paper had only four more days of life. The shock and bewilderment that came upon those reading the typed-out words of the official bulletin gave way to numbness, to fright, to muted bitterness, and to explosive anger, depending upon the individual. *The New York Sun* had been a great deal more than just a job to these men. It was a newspaper they had loved. They had stuck together for years in defying the Newspaper Guild and denying it a foothold in the organization; they had taken pride in *The Sun's* traditions, as they had in their own work and in their contributions to the independence and accuracy of the news stories. Many of them had stock in the paper and there were many who regarded it as a place that offered lifelong employment. Most of them had heard the management's ringing denial of sale rumors at an office dinner some years before and had remembered the exact words, "Yes, *The New York Sun is* for sale—at the newsstands for five cents!"

Not a man was impervious to the blow of that January

morning but a few tried to accept it cynically. It was a cyni-
cism, however, that was mingled with great uncertainty. Little
groups quickly formed in all parts of the city room and along
the second-floor corridors; there were scores of outgoing telephone calls. There was some forced laughter and a welling of
unchecked tears. There was some muttered snarling—"It's a
goddam outrage." "It's a tragedy, a tragedy." When the seventh
floor was so tactless and so insensitive as to call the extension of
one of the subeditors and ask what he thought of it all, that sub-
editor told off the top brass in stinging language, fixing full
responsibility for the catastrophe, which was certain to affect,
and adversely, the lives of many in the employee-personnel of
about a thousand.

Malcolm Johnson, who had won the Pulitzer Prize with
his stirring "Crime on the Waterfront" series, and who was
hidden away the day before to write the story of the paper's
passing, raged about the uselessness of *The Sun's* dying. A
copyreader from Oklahoma, not joining any of the chattering
groups, walked around in a daze, mumbling to himself. A
woman reporter of almost habitual gloom, who had somehow
foreseen and had even predicted the disappearance of the
paper, was red-eyed—and ready for the hearse. Jim Craig, the
chief editorial writer, graying and deaf and brilliant, a man of
eloquence when he rose to speak, was crushed and sickened;
he spent much of the day alone in his office, staring out upon
City Hall Park. Peter A. Dolan, one of the ablest of the editorial employees and long in the paper's service, was shaving
at his home in Brooklyn, just about ready to leave for the
office, and got the startling news by radio. But a half hour

later he sauntered in as he always had, outwardly nerveless and unruffled, but feeling it all deep in his heart. And there was the case of the office radical who went into something of a I-always-knew-they'd-sell-us-out tirade, and who later, within the privacy of Mr. Speed's office, put his head on the desk and wept bitterly.

By 3 P.M. of that day of *The Sun's* dying, numerous members of an excellent staff had obtained jobs, others had promises of jobs, and many others were still on the telephone. The news of the sale had spread quickly, and in no time the city desk was besieged by phone calls. Many old friends, unheard from for years, called up to offer sympathy. Photographers from newspapers and magazines swept into the city room and "shot" editors and reporters all day long to record the dying gasps of a great newspaper. In spite of all the turmoil, all the interference, all the distracting events, the men of *The Sun* continued at their tasks of getting out all the editions. Finally, the last edition went to press, but not before the men on the sports page had rushed into type the results of the last race from some winter track. The last form was locked up, the presses rolled for the last time, the final deliveries were sped through the streets in racing trucks—and *The Sun* was dead.

Many touching scenes were enacted as men who had worked together for years got their good nights for the last time. Every man on the paper made certain that he grasped Mr. Speed's hand and told him what a friend and a gentleman he had been. Although Mr. Speed was a member of *The Sun's* triumvirate, none blamed him for the death of the paper. The men of the editorial department felt that he was helpless and his voice powerless in the councils which decreed the paper's end. Women reporters and copy girls wept openly as they went to the desks of the city editor and the executive editor for their last good-bys. Men reporters went to the same desks, but their choking voices blocked the tributes they had intended to pay.

An ironical touch was added, a final humiliation, when City Editor Bartnett, on his way to the Chambers Street door at 4:30 P.M. to get into the taxi, Willie Schaefer's taxi, in which he always rode with Mr. Speed uptown, was stopped by a guard.

"Hey," said the man, "have you permission to take that from the building?" He indicated a large manila envelope under Bartnett's arm. The elevator starter identified the city editor and he was allowed to proceed.

By that time the paralyzing shock of the early morning had lessened to some extent and a communicable dejection had set in at 280 Broadway, a dejection that found expression in varying ways—in silence, in subdued laughter, in false light-heartedness, in sharp outbursts of bitterness, and in tears. There were tears, controlled tears, at the bar around the corner in Reade Street. There were uncontrolled tears later that evening at the New York apartment of Keats Speed and the Westchester home of Edmond Bartnett, who had been commuting between New Rochelle and City Hall Park for more than thirty years.

Something they both loved, something we all loved and respected and believed in and depended on, had passed into oblivion.

## chapter twelve

～～～～～～～～

THINGS have happened to me in New York, many things for which I'm grateful, others that I'm forgetting. In twenty-six years of daily column-writing I've turned out some 7,800,000 words, most of them having to do with the theater and its people. It's quite possible that I've found more sheer satisfaction in the writing of non-theater pieces, such as the exploration of Leopoldville, West Africa, and my discovery of La Paz, the 2-mile-high city gouged out of a ravine on the Bolivian altiplano, than I ever got from doing a play review or a high-powered interview in the Broadway area. It's also a little ironic that my infrequent stories of about-the-world wanderings always seem to bring forth a greater response than articles, even the best of the articles, about that badgered but still fighting institution, the great American theater. If I were asked, offhand, to name the play review in a decade of dramatic criticism that seemed to express most effectively what I'd wanted to say and had tried to say, I'd probably turn to the piece I did on Eugene O'Neill's *The*

*Iceman Cometh*, which ran for two full columns in *The New York Sun*. I was greatly impressed by that play; I was stunned when the principal actor, in his longest and most important speech, went up in his lines. But the impact of O'Neill's drama remained, and I had an exciting two hours at *The Sun's* lower-Broadway plant in the composition of the longest review I ever wrote. And then, some months later, and out of a perversity that seems to be a critic's occupational disease, I voted for Arthur Miller's *All My Sons,* in preference to *The Iceman Cometh,* as the best play of the season. I've always regretted such idiocy.

Taking stock, as of this moment early in 1953, I've put in a lot of hours at the typewriter since I first acquired the two-fingered knack in summertime practice sessions upon an old L. C. Smith in the offices of the Morehouse Manufacturing Company, city of Savannah. "The touch system is better," Miss Blanche Pacetti, my father's secretary, would say, "but I know you won't have the patience to do it that way." Besides those 7,800,000 words for my newspaper columns I've turned out numerous magazine articles, have had five books published, two plays produced on Broadway, received one-fourth royalties on a third, and another play was sold several times and finally got presentation in New Jersey. I was shocked at the time by the severity of a review published in the *New York World-Telegram,* a review based upon a ragged summer-theater performance, and it was a review so savage in its content that I lost all interest in the play and declined to do any rewriting. When I joined the staff of the *World-Telegram and Sun* ten years later I found that the man who had written the notice was sitting only a few desks away, but I hadn't retained any of that twenty-four hours of bitterness to which every playwright who gets an adverse notice is certainly entitled. The tall and courteous Mr. Norton Mockridge, an able rewrite man, who might have turned to theater-writing on his own account had he not been so expert in his city staff labors, has never mentioned *U. S. 90*, which began its career, and ended it, at the Paper Mill Playhouse, Millburn, N. J., and it's a subject that I certainly did not bring up.

My productivity as a writer would be far greater, in the line of books and plays, if I had been less inclined to get into a car and ride from ocean to ocean, less inclined to move across the world in flying machines, and perhaps less inclined to pick up wild animals in different parts of the world and bring them back to New York. I spent many hours in acquiring a lion cub in Johannesburg, even more hours in buying a Himalayan bear cub in Bangkok and in getting it past officials in Hong Kong and Tokyo and past our own diligent and literal-minded inspectors in Hawaii, and into the United States via San Francisco. If I've developed something of a living-on-borrowed-time philosophy, it's been brought about by use of the airplane and the motorcar for three decades. I never expected to survive a harrowing flight from New York to Cleveland, in which the plane took such a severe beating in a storm most of the passengers signed a petition calling upon the pilot to make a landing just anywhere, in a field or on a lake or a mountaintop. I'll never forget two hours of terrified flying during an electrical storm between Accra, on the Gold Coast of West Africa, and Leopoldville—several of us got whisky from the purser and drank it straight—and there was, some years before, a terrible crack-up in Chile, on a northward flight from Santiago, that brought me close to death. That was in 1931. Cliff Travis, Pan American pilot, at the controls of one of those ungainly trimotored Fords, had brought me through the 12,000-foot passes of the Andes without a mishap, but in making a routine landing in the blazing sunlight at the Chilean town of Ovalle he struck a cross-wind, his ship yawed, the tip of a wing scraped a stone fence, and the plane crashed. Three motors were torn off, Captain Travis was injured, and I sustained a severe gash in the right ankle. The Chileans who swarmed about the wreckage couldn't understand how any of us got out alive.

The next day an operations executive of Pan American–Grace flew into Ovalle, shuddered at the sight of the wreckage, turned to William I. Van Dusen, Leo Keiran, and myself, and snapped, "The mail's got to go through. I suppose you gentlemen would now prefer to get on a boat or something, but if you are still ready to fly we'll get you to Panama in a hurry. You'll ride with Harry Colliver, one of our best pilots, in a single-motored Lockheed. It's fast and he can fly."

Well, it was fast and he did fly—much of it at night, at low altitudes and guided by the light of the moon. Those were scary hours and my ankle began to get painful. By the time we reached Lima it was swelling, and in Miami I was ordered to a hospital. I stayed for three days, flew on to New York, and went immediately to my own doctor, Louis A. Wolfe. "My God," he said, as he looked at the leg, "what did they sew you up with—a horse needle?" He took out the stitches, treated the wound, put strips across it, and then he said, "You'll have to stay off that leg for three weeks. It's a wonder you didn't lose it."

Three weeks later Dr. Wolfe said, "Okay. You better stay out of airplanes." The next afternoon, while playing softball in Liberty Avenue, New Rochelle, just opposite the home of two old friends, Edmond and Helen Bartnett, I went racing for a fly, slipped off the high sidewalk curb, and fractured my *left* ankle. The star spectator of that afternoon was Miriam Hopkins. She came to me as I writhed upon the ground and, in her own devastatingly sympathetic fashion, said, "Oh, my God, what have you done *now?*"

Since I moved to New York three decades ago I've known many hours of the company, the delightful company, of some of the world's great people—unforgettable hours with Alfred Lunt and Lynn Fontanne in New York and in Genesee Depot, Wisconsin, a short visit with Sir James Barrie in London, a day or so with Booth Tarkington in Kennebunkport, and a crab-stew luncheon with H. L. Mencken in Baltimore. I have cherished every moment of an evening spent with William E. Borah in Washington, and I sat on the edge of Alfalfa Bill Murray's bed in a frighteningly dingy room in a Tishomingo (Oklahoma) hotel and disregarded his spitting upon the floor and upon the wall as he clawed his scalp and talked fascinatingly of the lore of Oklahoma and the Indian Territory. I found great satisfaction in my years of knowing, and seeing, George M. Cohan; I liked him enormously and had great admiration and respect for his limitless talent and for his contributions to the stage. I took up the job of writing his biography with some excitement, feeling that it would take the form of chapter after chapter of endless tribute to a revered song-and-dance man, to a beloved figure of the theater of our time. But as I went along with my research, and my writing, I was saddened by the realization that the Yankee Doodle Dandy, for all of his triumphs, would have to be presented as a bitter and disillusioned showman, as one who never recovered from the overwhelming defeat he suffered during the Equity Strike, when he was at the height of his prestige and popularity, and who had become an ineffectual figure in a changing American theater he didn't understand and no longer liked.

I have no regrets at all over several years of island-owning in the St. Lawrence River, and the time spent in trying to adapt myself to the summertime life in the Thousand Islands and adjust myself to the perils of shoals, storms, tides, currents, depth, tour boats, and lake freighters—and to the intricacies of marine engines, pumps, valves, fire extinguishers, buoys, blinkers, and channel markers.

Drinking was a problem to me for several years, just as it got to be to many who had their first taste of the stuff during prohibition years. I was fortunate enough to see it as a problem and it can never be again. I can still get mad every time I think of the $1200 that eight tormentingly dull weeks at the Institute of Living at Hartford, Connecticut, cost me, and during which time I was supposed to go in for an organized routine and attend daily classes that would bring about life-long abstinence. Classes in clay modeling and cooking, advanced Spanish and horticulture, squash and swimming and music appreciation. I was visited at regular intervals by a staff psychiatrist until he gave me up as utterly uncooperative and I refused to attend any classes except those at the swimming pool. I wasn't molested, read more than I had at any period in my life since I was fourteen, and made some progress in memorizing *Hamlet* line for line. On the day that I said good-by to the Hartford Retreat I had two drinks on the way to the railroad station and six more at the Ritz bar after I reached New York, all in a spirit of childish rebellion and to show the Institute that it had by no means effected a "cure." It's been my feeling on the drink problem that every man must be his own judge of his capacities and make his own decisions as to the penalties of drinking too much, or of drinking at all. I had a loathing for the Retreat during every hour that I spent there, but I did and do concede that those eight weeks had put me to thinking about the subject a great deal and had contributed to my making an important decision. In the late summer of 1944, just as the new theatrical season was under way and as I was about to leave for the theater to cover the season's first play, I looked at myself in the mirror and spoke these words, "I had a lousy summer. It cost me a lot of dough and it was no fun. I may have future troubles from time to time in my life, but I'll never again be bothered by overdrinking." And I never have been.

I've always regarded Atlanta as the most dramatic and unpredictable of cities, as a great Southern crossroads that is unfailing in its production of news, unexcelled as a source of almost continuous excitement of one kind or another. Perhaps I should have known all along that it would be in Atlanta that I would meet the person who has affected my life so deeply and who has made me a much happier man.

I went to dinner at the beautiful home of George C. Biggers and he told me of the fine staff he had at the *Journal;* he gave particular comment to the work of Rebecca Franklin, a south-Georgia girl, who had been invaluable as a general reporter for several years and had won great response from the farming areas of the state for her writings of the activities of the 4-H clubs. Mr. Biggers's remarks were recorded in my notebook—I'd gone to see him on an assignment from my good friend, James Wright Brown, president of *Editor & Publisher*—and the case of Miss Franklin was thereupon closed. A girl, I thought, who was undoubtedly satisfied with the local setup and who would eventually wear herself out in the Atlanta grind. The next day, however, as I sat in the *Journal's* morgue checking through some biographical clippings on Mr. Biggers, a trim and pretty blonde entered—quiet-voiced, unhurried, preoccupied, professional. She spoke to one of the attendants, received an envelope, and looked over a batch of clippings for some five minutes. Then she rose, mumbled her barely audible thanks, and was gone; she could not have been aware that I was even in the room, some thirty feet away. Having told myself early in life that I was more or less irresistible to women, I now wondered what had become of the sorcery that should have drawn at least a glance in my direction. I went to a member of the morgue staff—to the worker named Pauline, I believe—and, as I still flipped through the Biggers clips, and achieved what I felt was an effect of disinterest, I said casually, "That girl who was just in here—is she a *Journal* reporter?" Pauline looked at me a little incredulously. Then she said, "Why, of course. That was Rebecca Franklin, our Rebecca Franklin." And she watched me for my reaction to such an announcement.

That was enough. So that was the girl whose reporting and writing had so pleased the publisher-president. That was the darling of the 4-H clubs, the small, slight, golden-haired staff member from the yellow-pine country who could also cover fires, riots, Ku Klux Klan parades, wrecks, murders, floods, and sessions of the State legislature. So beauty plus brains had come in upon the Atlanta city room since my own days along Forsyth Street. Well, I wanted to meet Miss Franklin. I said so to my old friend Angus Perkerson, editor of the *Journal's* extraordinarily readable Sunday magazine and who had become brisker, quicker, sharper, and definitely younger with the passing of the years. Sure, drawled Perk, he was certain it could be arranged and that Miss Franklin would take boundless delight in meeting a famous *Journal* alumnus, and he thought I would be pleased with Miss Franklin because she was a real nice girl and awfully smart, but he just thought, perhaps, that Mrs. Perkerson had better attend to it all. Mrs. Perkerson got to the telephone and spoke quite a piece. It would be fine if Rebecca would come out to the Atlanta Biltmore to lunch the next day; she couldn't fail to like and enjoy Mr. Morehouse. Of course, he had been married and he *was* a little wild, but he had done fine work for the *Journal* a long time ago, just about the time General Sherman came through, and it would all be very nice and proper, what with both Perkersons at lunch and everything, and they just wouldn't take no for an answer.

Sorry, said Miss Franklin. Very sorry. But she was driving home for the week end; it was a long drive and she would have to leave at lunchtime to get there before dark. It would be nice to meet Mr. Morehouse at another time. Didn't he have a way of getting down to Atlanta every now and then?

Mrs. Perkerson telephoned me this report and I declined to accept it. "Give me her number," I said, "and I'll see if I'm as good with a telephone as I was when I was working for Harllee Branch."

So I called and I talked . . . and talked. It wasn't easy, but finally she gave up. We all had lunch at the Biltmore.

I was quite captivated by Becky Franklin. I went on back to New York and began a high-powered courtship that combined deep-South touches with a definitely northern technique. There was a letter to Atlanta daily, along with telegrams, flowers carefully timed, and at least one telephone call a day. Several weeks later Becky Franklin yielded to my urgings and flew to New York for a week end, something of a trip of inspection. There was no engagement by this time; there had been no commitments and no promises. I'm sure that she had been filled with a great surge of curiosity, that she desired a better and longer look at me, and she undoubtedly decided that three days in New York would blow it all up and that she could again give full time to her work and her friends, who had been recently neglected. They were complaining, too.

Ten minutes after Becky had checked into her hotel I had her at *South Pacific,* always the first stop on the grand tour of Broadway for favored visitors. The first person she met in New York was Walter Winchell, who was standing alongside us in the aisle, 44th Street side. We saw *South Pacific* to the final curtain, went on over to Twenty-One, and then to the Stork and El Morocco. Becky came away from the Stork with the regular souvenirs; she had drunk Mr. Billingsley's champagne but was still able to see Mr. Perona's zebra stripes, and she was still making sense, along with telling me that she really didn't like New York and could never dream of living in such a place, when we quit at 4 A.M. The next day I gave her a small luncheon party, took her on a round of the matinees, then to a cocktail party, and then suggested Westport for dinner—a good fifty miles away—and Becky was just about dead before we started. But she thought the country air would be good for her, and thought it would be a good idea to get out of steamy, sticky, sweltering New York.

Well, on the way to Westport I fell asleep at the wheel for the first time in all my years of driving and came near wrecking the car and killing us both as we ran off the parkway. We finally reached the home of my Westport friend and Becky agreed that the house was just as attractive as I'd said it was. But three of the guests were drunk, good and drunk, and she was soon wishing she could get back to Atlanta and was wondering why she had ever come North at all. I went with her to the Pennsylvania Station the next afternoon, rode with her as far as Philadelphia. She was obviously relieved when I stepped onto the platform and her train inched forward, southbound; I'm sure that she was overjoyed when she entered her snug Peachtree Street apartment in Atlanta the next morning. The nightmare was over. She was home, home, home!

But I thought, and thought correctly, that by the second day of her return she would be finding Atlanta a bit dull and would be thinking of the great whirl she had had and how really attentive I had been, and when there was no telegram, no letter, no telephone call from me for two days, for three days—all part of my hellish and deliberate scheming—she'd begin to think of me a great deal, to wonder if she could really live in New York, if she could possibly get to work on a paper or a magazine there, and just what sort of husband I would turn out to be. On Friday morning—Becky had now been back in Atlanta five days—I typed out a long and carefully worded wire, saying just what I wanted to say, and went with it to the Western Union office in the Grand Central Station. Two women were on duty. One of them had the look of a kindly soul and to her I said, "This telegram is just about the most important I ever sent in my life. It will either get this girl—or it won't. Please read it and tell me, from a woman's point of view, if there's anything I've left unsaid." She read the message; her hand trembled. She smiled and I thought she actually brushed away a tear. She counted the words, did a bit of addition, and then she spoke: "Mister, let it go as it is. I only wish I could get a telegram like that just once before I die. . . . $4.40, please."

A week later I was on an airplane, flying nonstop to Atlanta. Becky met me with her car at the airport. "Hello, darling," she said and threw her arms about me. "Everything is all set. Mother took it beautifully. We're going to the farm right now and we'll be married tomorrow afternoon and then we'll go to your beautiful De Soto in Savannah. . . . Come on, get in. We've got a drive of more than 200 miles."

"What about your apartment? Your job? Have you told the *Journal*?"

"I didn't dare. I wouldn't think of giving them a chance to talk me out of it. I'll telephone tomorrow morning and resign —from south Georgia. . . . Do you still want me to live with you in New York?"

That was Becky. That was the sound, sensible, reasoning Becky, giving up her Atlanta career, quitting a job that she had loved for eight years, walking out on an apartment mate to whom she was devoted, giving it all up for the precariousness of the North that she had somehow dreaded, for the uncertainty of marriage with a man she had seen for only a few hours in her life.

I realized that there was a spirit of adventure in Becky, along with her goodness, a touch of pleasant lunacy along with her wisdom and depth and decency.

We rode southward. The August twilight faded ever so slowly; darkness came upon a formless countryside. Becky was at the wheel of her big Buick, driving swiftly and deftly along the uncongested Georgia highways, glimmering like black glass in the moonlight. She took short cuts that she knew, a few shorter cuts that she didn't, circled the courthouses in the town squares, tore along the straightaways, and kept a watchful eye for spectral objects, such as unlighted and creeping farm vehicles, in going into the curves. A breeze swept in from the tall pines and caught up Becky's golden ringlets; the moon was copperish as it hung in the faintly star-flecked sky; pin points of light waxed into windows of farmhouses, hulking at the roadside, as we sped along. A juke box whined in a neoned beer stand and shrill laughter rose above it, and on down the highway a queue of Negroes shuffled into an old country church, warped and lopsided and wanly lighted, but still in the service of the Lord.

On we went, following route numbers that Becky well knew—on through Covington and Eatonton, Milledgeville and Swainsboro; on through the little town of Metter, nicely laid out around a park, and soon a turnoff from the main highway, a few more miles over a bumpy country road, a sharp turn-in at a gate, and then up to the front of an attractive house with a silvered roof and sturdy, red-brick pillars. Becky was home, back at her birthplace, back at the Franklin farm, near the hamlet of Register and in the county of Bulloch, home with the man she was to marry the next day. There were shrieks from the big front veranda as Mother and Brother appeared; hugs and kisses for Becky, greetings that seemed hearty enough for the Stranger. Something of a dubious choice, I must have appeared as they looked me over during the prodigious midnight supper. Not overage, necessarily, but undoubtedly overweight. Not of the physique of a commando or a lumberjack, not of a profile perfectly chiseled; a little deaf in one ear, a little sightless in one eye, but there was one redeeming factor: I was born in Georgia, even though I lived in New York. Then, too, my flow of midnight chatter, fresh from the damyankee country, amused Brother H. notwithstanding the fact that he was greatly agitated at the thought of losing his sister. And I found the audience of my life in the bright-eyed and sharp-eared Negro girl, Cooter, who had grown up on the Franklin farm. It's possible that a quick ten dollars made Cooter just a little more susceptible to my wiles and my small talk than she might have been ordinarily, but I shall always prefer to think that she is a creature of remarkable perception. In an hour or so after my arrival she delivered her verdict. "Miss Becky," she said, "has done gone and got herself a man."

I'd been told that it would be a quiet farm wedding. I'm sure that Becky meant it when she said it. But by four o'clock the next afternoon—the big day was a Saturday—all the people of Bulloch County seemed to be converging upon the Franklin property. Cars, cars, cars—shiny new ones, sturdy old ones— came along in an unceasing parade. Quiet home wedding! The Franklin place had suddenly taken on the tumult of a camp meeting merged with a county fair. Then the photographers began arriving like so many locusts and they were soon all over the house and in the living room and in the rosebushes.

I looked, trembled, and fled. I shut myself in the big front room, took a bottle of California port from the mantelpiece, put there by the thoughtful Becky for just such an emergency, and tried to lose myself in the It-Pays-to-Increase-Your-Word-Power exercises from an old *Reader's Digest*. When that failed me I turned to a favorite novel out of the long ago, George Barr McCutcheon's *Nedra*, and was actually reading it when Brother H., quite dressy in his high starched collar and his

Sunday best, entered and said, "Time to go, boy. We don't want to keep the preacher waitin'. . . . Just come with me."

Three hours later Becky and I left the Franklin farm, en route to Savannah. Two days later we boarded the *Silver Meteor* for New York. I had robbed the Franklins and the city room of the *Atlanta Journal*; I'd taken away Mr. Biggers's best reporter and the pride of the 4-H clubs, but I needed her more than they did.

## chapter thirteen

~~~~~~~~~~~~~~~

OF ALL the great people of the theater that
I have known, Gertrude Lawrence, who died late in 1952, was
the star who found the utmost excitement in the mere fact
that she was alive. Her joyous appreciation of life was expressed
in many ways. To the world, she was the essence of glamour
and sophistication, but she was supremely happy grubbing
away in old clothes in her Cape Cod rose garden; she liked to
paint rooms, wash windowpanes, rewire sockets, and knit
mittens, whether she was making them for Bernard Shaw or
for a friend just down the road. She enjoyed sewing, cooking,
finger painting, bicycle riding, swimming, sun-bathing and
collecting sea shells, a hobby acquired at Naples, Florida, during the last years of her life.

But those of us who had the good fortune to know her agree
that she found her greatest delight in giving, not only her
brilliant talent for theater, but also her time, her energy, her
money. One of her most endearing characteristics was what
Noel Coward has called her "insane generosity," and her life's

record is illumined by countless shining examples of thought-ful and tender concern for others. She found it almost impos-sible to refuse anybody anything. "I never saw her refuse any-body an autograph, even when she was terribly tired after the show," says William Hood, her chauffeur for many years. "She never got too big for her public."

Hood, as she called him, always knew rainy nights meant extra riders. If there were people huddled beneath the mar-quee unable to get cabs when he and Miss Lawrence left the theater, she would sing out gaily, "Anybody going my way?" Those who accepted were driven home before she went home herself. She was warned many times that this was a dangerous practice, but she never discontinued it.

Miss Lawrence was the easiest mark for a touch the theater has known since George M. Cohan's day. Early in the run of *The King and I,* her last and perhaps biggest success, a man took up a position night after night in the St. James's stage-door alley, standing with his back against the wall, his cap in outstretched hand. And night after night she stopped long enough to drop a bill or some coins into his cap. Finally, after weeks of this, she became a little exasperated. "Now, listen, you," she said, pausing alongside him. "This has become a racket and I don't want to find you here any more. Here—go out and get yourself a job." She handed him twenty dollars. A few weeks later, the doorman gave her an envelope which contained a dollar bill and this scrawl, "I got a job. Here's a buck on my account."

She was peculiarly sensitive to the financial woes of down-and-out actors and actresses; a friend who knew her for thirty years says the loans she gave such people are "beyond estimation." There was a long list of people in England to whom she sent food packages every month. The flowers sent to her by admirers were inevitably passed along to hospitals, usually to children's wards. Any friend who was hospitalized could always count on a deluge of flowers and gifts from "Gee." She was a lavish tipper around the theater and at her apartment house. When she was on tour, at every hotel stop there were five-dollar tips all around, even for the maids, telephone operators, and elevator boys who are usually overlooked.

She remembered birthdays and anniversaries, but she also gave impulsively. There was the time on a bitterly cold morning at Cape Cod, when she went to see Dorothy Hood, her maid and companion for twenty years, off on the train from Yarmouth to New York. Without saying a word, she reached over and pinned Dorothy's collar more snugly, using her own beautiful brooch. Dorothy, who cannot talk of Miss Lawrence without tears, was never permitted to return it.

The Christmas season was Gertrude Lawrence's as much as it was any child's. She adored Christmas. The gifts which she began piling up in September—two, three, and sometimes four for every friend, and at least one for every member of her company—took three frenzied days for Hood to deliver, but he grew to love it. She took great pleasure in wrapping each parcel and in addressing the cards, and she would go to any trouble or expense to find a gift she thought would please the recipient. She scoured New York once for a cane for Alexander Woollcott. He had a great collection and she wanted to give him one he didn't have. She finally found one after much searching. The price: one hundred dollars. But she was just as interested in seeing that the man who patrolled her block got a cashmere sweater and that the boys who gassed and polished her car received a cash remembrance.

Perhaps the meager Christmases she knew as a child had something to do with her extravagant delight in Christmas. But the biggest factor was her warm and loving heart. Once, while she was touring in Noel Coward's *Tonight at 8:30*, she had a special car put onto the train on Christmas Eve—and on that car there was a glittering Christmas tree loaded from top to bottom with presents for the company from "Gee." (Her old friends called her Gertie, but it was a name she grew to dislike in later years, preferring instead "Gee" or simply Gertrude.)

"When you begin enumerating all the wonderful things there were about Gertrude," one of her oldest friends said to me, "she begins to sound Pollyanna-ish, and she wouldn't like that at all. She was a dynamic person with a tremendous basic drive, and she never set herself up as the friend of mankind or anything like that. She didn't court the affection and approval of people. But she loved people and something shone out of her that drew people to her."

Gertrude Lawrence was irrepressibly gay. She had a flashing wit and a sense of humor. Even on serious occasions there was a glint of mischief in her eyes. In her early years, when she was playing in *Charlot's Revue* in London, she and Beatrice Lillie became the scourge of the company by reason of the outrageous practical jokes they played. She lost her taste for pranks of that sort, but she never lost her flair for the comic.

Noel Coward, whom she first met at a children's dancing

school in England, was probably her favorite sparring partner. For forty years, across many a dazzled dinner table, by long distance telephone, and by telegraph, they kept up a bantering, teasing, mocking but always affectionate friendship. When in 1929 she appeared in *Candle Light*, her first nonmusical play, Coward wired her tauntingly, "Legitimate at last, darling, won't mother be pleased?" After she was married to Richard S. Aldrich, the theatrical producer, in a candlelit ceremony held at Cape Cod a few minutes after midnight on her birthday, July 4, 1940, she received this message.

> Dear Mrs. A.
> Hooray, hooray,
> At last you are deflowered,
> On this as every other day
> I love you. . . . Noel Coward.

This actress of the international theater never wanted anybody to see her when she wasn't at her best; thus people got the idea that she was gay all the time. Actually, she was quite quiet at home and had a melancholy streak which cropped up occasionally, but which she kept resolutely to herself. She never wallowed in trouble or made a public show of it. Nor was she one to display temper for the world to see. I never heard of any instance, during the twenty-odd years I knew her, of her getting mad with a stagehand, a doorman, a cab-driver, or a waiter. "During the year and a half I knew her," says young Sandy Kennedy, who created the role of Anna's son in *The King and I*, "I never heard her say a disagreeable word to anyone."

This same Sandy gave her a doll's house which was in her dressing room at the St. James at the time of her death. It was the only doll's house she had ever owned.

Miss Lawrence was proud of being a star and of her position in the theater, but she retained her simplicity; aloofness and conceit were not in her make-up. She was never completely separated from her cockney upbringing. For all of her fame, her steady rise to success, and the love of countless friends, her life was not all ease and pleasantness. She knew uncertainty and insecurity during her childhood years in London's Clapham; she had agonizing moments during her first marriage (to Francis Gordon-Howley), which didn't work out; and after she was an established star she experienced the pride-shattering ordeal of a British bankruptcy court, which seized her cars, her apartment, her jewels, and most of her clothes. She worked two years, carrying on three jobs simultaneously (the movies in daytime, the stage at night, and a night-club singing stint afterward) to pay off her debts. But she did it.

Through it all, she retained her zest, her spirit, her cheerfulness, and a philosophy of making the best of things. It was a philosophy that had expression in one of her favorite cockney sayings, "You pays your money and you takes your chances." She never learned to be thrifty. "I know I am foolish about money. Some women are," she once said. "I do not have a true sense of its value." In later years, her financial affairs were handled by David and Fanny Holtzman, New York lawyers, and she was kept on a strict allowance.

No stage beauty was Gertrude Lawrence. She had an overlarge nose, and she often laughed about it. She didn't have a great voice, but there was something poignant and memorable about the way she sang a song. And as she remarked to me a few years after she had enchanted New York in *Charlot's Revue*, "I never was any great shakes as a dancer." Yet no one who saw *The King and I* will ever forget her lissome grace as she whirled through the "Shall We Dance?" number with Yul Brynner. Her talent was described as "kaleidoscopic" by Noel Coward, who went on to say, "On the stage she is potentially capable of anything and everything. She can be gay, sad, witty, tragic, funny, and touching." She was indeed a very rare creature in our theater of today: a singer, a dancer, a comedienne, and a dramatic actress. For me she had magic and glamour in the real sense of the word. Above all, she was an absolute pro.

Self-improvement is an old-fashioned virtue and Gertrude Lawrence believed and practiced it implicitly. Sometimes with rather amusing results. During the run of *Private Lives*, there were stories of off-stage battles between Miss Lawrence and Noel Coward, who had written the comedy especially for her. There came a matinee when she played the love scene exactly as Coward wanted it played. After the final curtain he rushed to her and told her how right she had been, how touched he was, how happy she had made him. Miss Lawrence was enormously pleased and bowed shyly. In the performance that evening, when the love scene was reached, she went into a complete reversal of form, giving way to all the artificialities he had worked so hard to make her drop. Coward was in a rage when they left the stage but before he could scream at her she turned to him with an eager smile and said, "Better, darling?"

During the last summer of her life she took voice lessons and learned the role of Mimi in *La Boheme*. She was also learning French and writing a book on acting. When she was still a teen-ager, she noticed that some of the girls in shows with her "did not hear that insistent, not-to-be-ignored inner drive which forced me to practice constantly and to learn more and always more about the theater." She added, in her autobiography, "I cannot take any credit to myself for this determination to succeed, for it was inherent in my nature. I did have to battle through periods of despair and frustration. But I am by nature hopeful. I do not understand defeat."

Gertrude Alexandra Dagmar Lawrence Klasen, daughter of a Danish actor-singer, Arthur Lawrence Klasen, and his English wife, Alice Louise Banks, a small-part actress, was born in Kennington Oval, London, within the sound of Bow bells. Her parents separated while she was an infant, and she grew up with a kind but impecunious stepfather. She danced in the streets of Clapham to an organ-grinder's tunes, and she thrilled to the fortune foretold for her by a penny-in-the-slot machine during an excursion to Brighton. Her destiny read, "A star danced, and you were born."

She was still a thin, gawky child, sallow of complexion and given to chest colds, when she played her first role on the stage. She knew immediately what she wanted, because soon, with sublime self-confidence, she was passing out business cards which announced, "Little Gertie Lawrence—Actress and Danseuse." She never regretted that decision, and from the age of about fourteen onward she made her own way in life on the stage, and with her earnings was at one time supporting her mother, her own father, her stepfather, and her grandmother.

"One reason why I have always loved the theater," she said later, "and why I'm still stage-struck is that this sort of life offers variety, constant change, even dangerous and thrilling ups and downs. At heart I have always been an adventurer. The Danish strain in my blood makes me restless. I am a seeker, not a holder. I am filled with urgent curiosity about what may lie just around the corner."

She made contributions to the stage of New York and London which are unforgettable. There was her "Limehouse Blues" song from *Charlot's Revue* and her "Jenny" from *Lady in the Dark;* there was her touching "Someday I'll Find You" from the otherwise tempestuous *Private Lives.* Her versatility was tested in a wide range of roles—the slatternly, nagging cockney wife in Coward's *Fumed Oak* and the bouncy music-hall entertainer in his *Red Peppers;* the vain, destructive, and exhibitionistic Susan in *Susan and God;* the opportunistic Liza Doolittle in Shaw's *Pygmalion;* the tired and neurotic editor of a woman's magazine in Moss Hart's *Lady in the Dark.* And in *The King and I,* Miss Lawrence played, and played superbly, some quiet, tender, Anna-and-the-King scenes that tore at the heart.

Her complete dedication to the theater amazed Moss Hart after rehearsals for *Lady in the Dark* got under way. "Sensitive and kind and completely conscientious, I would have to drive her out of the theater at night," he says. And he adds, "There was one element in the working relationship with Gertie that I have never experienced in working with any other actress.

218

That element was fun." She was never late for a rehearsal or a performance; in fact, she usually showed up at the theater two hours before curtain time.

Her buoyant spirit lifted the morale of every company she worked with. "It was a lovely thing she gave to us," said an actress who toured with her in *Tonight at 8:30*. "Before the curtain went up, she would beam at us gaily and say, 'Come on, boys and girls, we're going to have fun—and they're going to have fun!'" Little Johnny Connoughton, who plays one of the children in *The King and I*, wrote recently, "Miss Lawrence was like a real mother to me. Every night before the curtain went up, she would check my make-up and my costume, and she would call it inspection. I loved her as much as my own mother. I learned many tricks from her about the theater." The performance following her death was a heartbreaking one for her company, but as Yul Brynner said, "If she could have spoken to us, she would have said, 'All right now, boys and girls, a little smile please—and let's get on with it.'"

Miss Lawrence always retained her British citizenship—"one doesn't give up one's country" was a frequent statement from her on that subject. And she never actually established a home for herself in America until her marriage to the quiet, unruffled, extraordinarily gracious Richard S. Aldrich, a Bostonian, Harvard man, and banker turned producer. After the break-up of her first marriage, she had many suitors and there were at least two engagements, but as she herself said, "Richard was the first man who understood what my career in the theater meant to me—the first man who really understood me." He brought to her life the stability and security it had previously lacked. Her closest friends say it was a happy marriage and that she adored him.

Certainly after their marriage she lost interest in the social activities which had consumed a lot of her time. She rarely went to parties and she was seldom seen any more in the smart restaurants and supper clubs. There was even a slackening of her interest in clothes, although in the past she was several times named among the ten best-dressed women and, during one period of hectic social endeavor, she bought a new Hattie Carnegie dress for every party—even when there were four and five parties a week. She remained chicly dressed, but somehow clothes did not seem so important any more.

Gertrude Lawrence died of cancer. Death came to her just a short time after she had completed, at Cape Cod, a six-week holiday that had seemed the most health-giving of her entire life. Sun-browned, alluring, and so very alive, she returned to New York toward the end of a week, saw a performance of *The King and I* at a Saturday matinee, and returned to the cast the following Monday. Stoically, and with her accustomed gallantry, she went through the week suffering an almost unbearable pain and was unable to appear for the Saturday evening performance. Then, on the following Tuesday, she went into the hospital, where her illness was diagnosed as acute hepatitis. An examination following her death showed a "primary tumor of the liver."

Death came to Gertrude Lawrence at the high tide of her career. She was denied two things she very much wanted, attending the coronation of Queen Elizabeth II and appearing in *The King and I* in the city of her birth. ("I belong to London as each of us can belong to only one place on earth. And, in the same way, London belongs to me.") But she closed out her life with her best performance in the finest play she ever had, playing the role of Anna Leonowens, a woman strangely like herself in courage and warmth of heart.

Letters and telegrams poured in upon Richard Stoddard Aldrich from the great of the world and from little people, from those who had known her well, or slightly, or not at all, except as an electric presence across the footlights. They came from doormen and cabdrivers and ushers, from stagehands, wardrobe women, gallery gods. Adlai Stevenson wrote a letter and so did David Niven, Marlene Dietrich, Helen Hayes, and Beatrice Lillie; the Duke of Windsor, a long-time friend, sent a cable and so did Laurence Olivier. These letters, these wires, hundreds and hundreds of both, provide an astounding revelation of the impact she had upon people in many walks of life, in many parts of the world.

Big black headlines screamed the news of her passing from the front pages of newspapers around the world. Many carried eloquent editorials. *The New York Times* said, "It was her peculiar gift to make herself seem personally known to everyone who watched her and listened to her. This was more than merely what is called 'projecting a personality.' It was making of the theater a living experience in which the audience was invited to share. It was an experience of enormous gusto, of joy in life, of constant variety, and unchanging warmth." The *Journal-American* said simply, "Goodby, Gertie. You made life happier while you were part of it. We shall never see the like of you again."

A heartbroken Noel Coward cabled, "I shall miss her as long as I live." John Mason Brown wrote, "Life for her was an unending show and she always gave a good one, giving it everything she had." Ed Sullivan called her "a shimmering, glittering ornament on the theater's Christmas tree." And from Beverly Nichols in London came these words, "Gertie's death is going to make a whole lot of us feel somehow older overnight."

Not in my experience has any person of the stage received such loving and heartfelt homage. At 8:30 P.M. on the day of her funeral, Broadway's incandescent glow was dimmed for one minute in her honor, as was London's famed Piccadilly across the sea. At Columbia University, where she had been a guest professor in the School of Dramatic Art, the flag was lowered to half staff. She had come a long way since the days of "Little Gertie Lawrence—Actress and Danseuse."

She lies today on a grassy knoll in Lakeview Cemetery at Upton, Massachusetts, in a plot which has belonged to the Aldrich family for more than two hundred years. It's a strange resting place, some think, for the blithe creature who was the toast of two continents. But I am inclined to agree with another friend of hers who said, "She might have giggled about being with Richard's Puritan ancestors, but actually she would have been very proud. You see, she loved being Mrs. Richard Aldrich."

## chapter fourteen

NEW YORK remains in 1953 what it was in 1903, the unchallenged theatrical capital of America. There has never been any threat of replacement, any possibility of dislodgment, but in the concentration of playhouses spread over a frenzied chunk of midtown Manhattan the drama is merely holding a beachhead on the continent. There are a few scattered outposts, such as Boston and Philadelphia and Chicago, San Francisco and Los Angeles, in which the theater asserts itself, but if you take a motor ride today from the Hudson to the Golden Gate there will be few indications, en route, that the professional theater is still with us, few reminders that it ever lived at all within the margins of North America.

When middle-aged people of the prairie states who knew and loved, in their youth, the resident stock companies get to finding life unendurable without sight or sound of actors walking around beneath a proscenium arch, Chicago, with its limited stage fare, is possibly not too far away. Sentimentalists in their forties and fifties living in the coast cities—Seattle, San

Francisco, Los Angeles—have come to know that they don't have to go hurtling eastward for their drama, that sooner or later the outstanding new plays will somehow get to them. Bostonians and Philadelphians are within commuting distance of Broadway, the drama's sanctuary, the region in which the theater holds its ground as it waits for the great upheaval, for the emotional rediscovery of the legitimate theater, which will again send the stock company and the touring company to all corners of the land. Until the theater finds a way of restoring the long-vanished industry that was known as The Road, people of Wichita and Corpus Christi, Tampa and Roanoke and Little Rock, Phoenix and Butte and Salt Lake City, will go along hardly missing a commodity that is seemingly non-existent, a form of entertainment that is seldom in their consciousness or within their reach.

The Broadway area of 1952–1953, in which the living theater makes its brave stand, remains a district that has all the manifestations of the midway and the honky-tonk—a harsh and clangorous theatrical center that is filled with the quackings and the yappings of the bus barkers and the sidewalk venders, the muttered snarls of cops and cabdrivers, the yawps and the giggles of the strolling neck-craners, the dronings of the cinema doormen. An area, God save it, of flower peddlers and hot-chestnut salesmen, of wheat cakes and nut fudge, fruit drinks and jumbo malts, of chop suey and hot waffles and hot dogs and ham and eggs, of rug auctions and gypsy tearooms and photos-while-U-wait. Bring on the roller coaster, turn on the Ferris wheel, and you're back at Coney Island. Broadway is all of that.

But it's also, God bless it, the fertile ground in which the imaginative and beautiful musical play blooms as nowhere else on earth and which brings forth, now and then, skillfully written and blissfully acted dramatic plays—the area of thirty or so outmoded but still serviceable legitimate theaters, the area in which actors get work (now and then), plays are sold, plays are cast, plays are rehearsed, plays are financed, plays are presented. Producers continue to take the big gamble, trying to earn an honest dollar in a risky and elusive business.

It's in the Broadway area, to the north of 40th Street and on into the mid-Fifties, that the New York theater settled, and with the decision to stay for a while, after moving northward from Herald Square and Madison Square, from the gaiety and congestion of Union Square, from the little streets of lower Manhattan, south of Canal, where the metropolitan drama had its nervous beginnings a matter of two hundred years ago. It's in the braying, brazen, midwayish, and blindingly lighted Broadway sector, as of 1953, that the American theater now displays its wares and invites playgoers from metropolitan New York, all of the suburban territory, and all of the forty-eight states, to step right up and put their money on the line. And to see live actors in plays that are mediocre, plays that are almost good, plays that are first-rate.

Broadway is a show window for some great and genuine talents; it is also a constricted, small-town center of house-to-house and block-to-block gossip, some of it playfully malicious, a lot of it destructively vicious. The Broadway scene is one of many acts of graciousness and benevolence, many demonstrations of decency and generosity, but it also knows much that is rancorous and retaliative. There is an emphasis on littleness in this highly competitive community; there is a great deal that is self-glorifying and ostentatious.

Broadway, with its feuds and enmities, jealousies and distrust, its venom and vindictiveness, along with its loyalties and trials and triumphs, is the area of the hearty but hollow greeting, the phony handshake, the unlistening ears, the unseeing eye-to-eye stares, and of the legends and the myths.

Broadway is the El Dorado (upon occasion) into which a showman can enter with a shoestring and depart a millionaire; also the glittering and rectangular portion of New York's real estate in which just one show, just one turn of the wheel, can cost a man $300,000—if he has been fortunate enough to have that kind of money and reckless enough to invest it all. In the Broadway world enthusiasms are fleeting, ratings are ever subject to change, mediocrity leads only to oblivion, and genius, once asserted and acclaimed, cannot falter; it must be sustained from season to season. An actor is as good as his last performance; a critic is loved, or is scorned, by his last notice. Broadway is the land of the transient friendship, the friendship of convenience.

I'll cite a case in point. I had a friend among the producers; a good friend, I thought. Had known him twenty years. Took a trip with him to the West Indies, another to London; went duck shooting with him in Canada and off the Virginia coast, and spent many summertime week ends at his beautiful country place. It was, and is, an estate with a long driveway, precisely margined and carefully kept; flower beds and green-

226

houses, great elms and rolling fields; a stable, a playhouse, a pool, and a barn as neat as a window at Saks Fifth Avenue.

On the inside of the house, everything was on the side of luxury and graciousness and comfort and well-being. The master's guns were shining beneath the glass of a beautiful made-to-order wall cabinet; the bathroom towels were exquisitely monogrammed; there was beautiful glassware all over the place, and porcelain and miniatures and mementos. The table linen was perfect, as was the cut glass and the silver. The steaks were thick and so was the cream; the eggs were fresh, the champagne was cold. I enjoyed those week ends.

But I don't go to that estate any more. My friend for twenty years isn't a friend any longer, and now I wonder if he ever was. The trouble was, he produced a play. It wasn't a good play and I said so very definitely. I don't know what he actually expected me to do, but he quit speaking for about eight months. Then, as it all seemed to be forgotten, there was again the hearty but hollow greeting, the firm but meaningless handshake. My estate-owning friend then produced another play, much worse than the other. I again reviewed it and I again expressed a frank opinion of it, as I would have done had it been written by my brother or my boss or my favorite aunt. This time, the gentleman from Connecticut got good and mad. He denounced me to his assembled company; he forbade my name to be mentioned at the dinner table. I have not set eyes upon him since that last notice appeared. If he produces another bad play, and if I am still functioning as a critic, I shall speak my piece about it, and with no reservations. If it is a good play I shall cheer it, and take great joy in doing so. But when the telephone rings, and I'm invited back to Connecticut, I shan't accept.

Dramatic critics, like many stage stars, have had their reigns —and their importance—in the theater of New York and America since the turn of the century. The critics, like the actors, are better paid than they used to be and a critic in 1953 has less work to do than those of his calling in the twenties, Broadway's production-peak decade. The critics, unlike the ladies and gentlemen of the acting profession, have never gone on strike. No such manifestation is foreseen for the next ten or twelve centuries.

Jobs in the field of dramatic criticism have become scarcer as the number of daily newspapers in America has undergone shrinkage. Only in New York, for nine months out of a year, is the reviewing post regarded as full-time work, and some executive editors in the metropolitan scene have been known to look upon the critic's job as the softest in the shop. A con- scientious fellow in this much-desired post is not averse to occasional off-Broadway reviewing. To justify his existence, and to protect and keep the franchise during the lulls in play production, he is quite likely to go in for a bit of travel and to report upon the state of the drama in Texas, in California, and in London. And several of the present-day New York critics have given a great deal of time and space to the operations of the summer-theater circuit. In many cities of our country the man who covers the road plays that turn up now and then is also the man who writes of movies and music and occasionally does odd jobs for the city desk.

It's my definite impression that the play reviews published

in New York City are sharper, tougher, and more decisive than those that appear elsewhere, but even as I make this observation I bow low to the well-written pronouncements of the outspoken Claudia Cassidy, who scares hell out of the actors in Chicago. I well realize that plays are frequently blasted by the Chicago press, and in Pittsburgh and Boston and Philadelphia, but I also certainly know that the dwindling of the road has created something of a tendency in the midlands to go just a little easy on attractions taking the great touring risk. I give you the comment of an estimable out-of-town critic, a man respected for his knowledge of the drama, who turned in a highly favorable notice on a weak play brought to his town by a big female star. "Listen," he said to me, "we get damn few plays; we have to be grateful for those we do get. I know that this play is no good, but if I kicked it around as you fellows in New York will probably do, I'd do nothing but get everybody mad and bring our theater just a little closer to putting in pictures or something for all the year round."

It's in New York as in no other city, the showmen tell me, that playgoers in general are inclined to rely upon the verdicts of the critics; it's in New York that a set of rave notices can cause an immediate stampede at a box office. But even in New York there are times when the press, completely unanimous in approval, fails to put over a play that the public doesn't want. Take the case of the 1951 revival of *The Green Pastures*. Thousands of words were written by the reviewers of the dailies and the periodicals in tribute to the enduring enchantment of the Marc Connelly fable, but all of this praise couldn't keep the revival running for more than a few weeks, didn't prevent a production loss of something in excess of $200,000. Cheers from the aisle seats for the writing and the acting in the Philip Barry-Robert E. Sherwood *Second Threshold* left the public apathetic. Bravos in the day-after reviews and in the follow-up week-end articles are enormously gratifying to authors, actors, and producers, as in the case of *Billy Budd*, but it is demonstrated in nearly every season that all-out critical support can't make a hit of a play to which there is some strange, massed, chemical resistance.

A theatergoing public not always willing—and it's the New York area that I have in mind—to take the word of the critics that such and such a play must not be missed is the same public that is seemingly quite ready to accept, and without question, a verdict of condemnation. All of which brings us to this established truth in the Broadway theater of this writing: the critics can't always turn a play into a smash hit, or even into a moderate success, but in ninety-nine times out of a hundred they can kill a play with a unanimously unfavorable decision. "It's the concentrated fire, all coming at once, and on the same day, that you can't fight against," Moss Hart once told me, in discussing the subject of the press vs. the theater. But he well knows that eight good notices for a play, and printed simultaneously, can generally create a half-block queue at the box office.

It's the contention of the stage-wise Max Gordon, producer of scores of plays, that outright damnation of a play from two of the New York morning papers, *The Times* and the *Tribune*, will force the closing of such a play—and quick. I mentioned to him, in rebuttal, the case of *The Heiress*, attacked with some severity by both *The Times* and the *Tribune* and it ran for a year. But you will find it difficult to name more than a few, in the course of an entire decade, that have prospered notwithstanding the *T-T* dissent. Would Mr. Gordon like to abolish criticism and have the verdict left entirely to the public? Would he like to try *not* inviting the press to his next opening? He doesn't feel that he will go in for such experimentation, but he would be interested to see the no-reviews idea tested by another management. Mr. Gordon, like most managers, is an optimist; he always believes that his next show will be one that will draw *Born Yesterday* notices.

Critics, along with the theater itself, have been subjected to stinging and intermittent attacks from the producers of New York ever since the chimes of Old Trinity rang in the new century. They've been given up as hopeless, from time to time, by such sagacious and influential showmen as Henry W. Savage and William A. Brady, Arthur Hopkins and Edgar Selwyn, A. H. Woods and Elmer Rice, and Maxwell Anderson. But the gentleman of the aisle seats, like Mother Goddam, have survived. No indication of their immediate passing is now apparent. The theater, in its present hit-or-nothing status, with costs remaining at frightening levels, has been having tough going for a decade, but there can be no lowering of critical standards if play reviewing is to continue to hold the respect of readers of newspapers and magazines. However inept or stupid a critic may seem to be in the opinion of a playgoer, the honesty of a review in the New York area is seldom, if ever, questioned.

The fact that some nice fellows have worked for two or three years to raise the money to put on a show costing $200,000 or $300,000 doesn't bring out even a suggestion of leniency from the seven experts (more or less) in the employ of that number of daily papers still published on the island of Manhattan—seven men holding jobs that thousands of others envy, would like to have, and for which they feel, deep in their hearts, that they have outstanding qualifications. It's the theater's task, of course, to reach the state of excellence demanded by those seven men of the dailies and the likes of them on the weeklies who get paid for seeing plays in free seats and then going to their typewriters and recording their impressions for print. The New York theater, in its moments of greatness, has no fear of the critics, most of whom go to the theater hoping that they will see something to cheer about. When such a thing as *The King and I* comes along the man in C 2–4 or D 1–3 thanks God that he didn't stay on in Sports or Books, and that he had the good sense, and the good fortune, to find a place in the dramatic department.

Present-day dramatic critics, besides being better paid than were their brethren of other decades, have less work to do because Broadway's production mill has slowed down perceptibly during the last two decades. A busy week in midseason of 1952–1953 was one that brought in four openings. During the frenzy of the twenties there were many nights on which four plays opened simultaneously. And all of us who have been following the theater for some years like to stand at the bar of Twenty-One and tell about the extraordinary evening of December 26, 1927, the night that gave the town exactly eleven plays!

232

Reviews of today are shorter than they were during the years of such august critics as William Winter (*Tribune*), Edward A. Dithmar (*Times*), James Gibbons Huneker (*Sun*), Acton Davies (*Evening Sun*). There is now a tendency to skim over the plot in a few sentences; in many reviews of thirty and forty years ago the mere recital of the story of a new play by Clyde Fitch or Augustus Thomas or Edward Sheldon would go on for nine or ten closely packed paragraphs. A New York play review published in this second half of an incredible century is much more likely to include a critic's sharply stated yes-or-no opinion than was a critique of 1911 or 1921. Perhaps the trend toward directness can be attributed, in part, to the influence of *Variety's* supposedly loathsome box score, reluctantly dropped by that publication after having established itself as a standard feature for more than two decades.

Many indecisive reviews appeared under the by-line of that impeccable stylist, Percy Hammond, who achieved his blissful and seemingly easy prose after an hour and a half of mental and physical torture. Hammond took his hefty frame to Manhattan's playhouses night after night during those seasons in the twenties that brought in swarms of plays, that produced some great dramatists, and that had some men of wit, sagacity, and writing skill in the critics' posts. I have in mind such men as George Jean Nathan, Brooks Atkinson, Richard Watts, Gilbert Gabriel, and John Mason Brown.

It's to the theater's great benefit, and a tribute to the durability of man, that four of these reviewers are still writing from the aisle seats, that they are still following what Mr. Atkinson has described as an "ignoble profession."

## *chapter fifteen*

~~~~~~~~~~~~

THREE decades of living in the uproar and
dissonance of the highly competitive Manhattan Island can
put you to wondering how you've done it and why you've done
it. You sometimes bemoan the fact that in a world of seemingly
greener pastures you must go along with the day-to-day frenzy
of an unsparing metropolis, a vertical and jangling warren of
stainless steel, shiny chromium, rush-hour mobs, and outrageous manners. And yet, you develop an affection for it all
and you get to defending New York as you berate it.

I have undoubtedly been inclined to regard myself as time-
less and ageless and somehow changeless—definitely a defen-
sive process to avoid any alarm that might be brought on by the
passing of the years—but I seem to have been told that life is
short and I've found no evidence to lead me to think otherwise.
I readily admit trying to crowd a lot into it.

Even though I've found comfort and excitement and many
good friends in New York and have always been eager to get
back to it after long absences, I've never actually planned to

remain a New Yorker for the rest of my days. After three decades of it, I've seen the elephant, as Lucius Beebe remarked in his retrospective comment, once he had removed himself to the objectivity and the new sensations of life in Virginia City, Nevada. My own feeling has been that there is so much that is attractive and fascinating in so many parts of the world, and certainly in our own incredible republic, I just don't want to live on and on in New York until I'm too venerable to battle for a taxi, climb the subway stairs, ride the escalator, or walk down a theater aisle. "I've loved living in this damned town," I told a skeptical visitor of recent months, "and I've never been bored here for five minutes, and I doubt if I could say that about any other place in the world, but the time will come when I'll want to spread myself around, I'll want to be foot-loose. New York's been great, but I'd never want to die here. Give me Danville, Virginia, say, or Tucumcari, New Mexico, or Atlanta. When my friends read about me on the page opposite the editorials I want the story to carry a date line."

Notwithstanding all my wanderings since I've called New York my home there are still yearnings in the line of getting out and seeing the world, and perhaps in the more or less whimsical category. I want to take a leisurely barge trip along the Mississippi, and without having to do a book about it, or even a batch of daily columns. I've long been eager to ride for a day tagging along at the end of a string of dreary freight cars in a bouncy and jolly-looking caboose. I've always wondered if the brakeman got in a lot of reading or carried along a radio or a television set; Lucius Beebe's caboose would be equipped, of course, with an icebox and there'd be fresh caviar and imported champagne. An extraordinarily interesting year could be put in touring the Civil War battlefields and, having been born in the realm of the Confederacy, I would want to linger overtime at Shiloh and at such sites of carnage and Confederate victory as Chancellorsville and Bull Run. Somehow, during the many years that are seemingly left to me, I shall want to crowd in a trip to Tierra del Fuego and to Afghanistan and go back to Green River, Wyoming, and spend a month trying to shoot quail in the broom sage near the beautiful little town of Manning, South Carolina.

If you have ever occupied one of those circular suites in Savannah's Hotel DeSoto and have been awakened by the soothing chimes from St. John's Episcopal Church across the square you will well understand my desire to return for a long enjoyment of the DeSoto's hospitality and comfort. I definitely feel that no travel-minded person has lived at all who hasn't spent some time in a river suite at London's Savoy or in quarters at Boston's Ritz-Carlton, with the jungle-green foliage of the public garden just on the other side of Arlington Street. And, of course, before I'm committed permanently to a wheel chair, I'd like to try that Alcan Highway to Alaska and gaze once more upon the Jungfrau from a terrace in Interlaken and return to La Paz, that slanting city on the Bolivian altiplano, where people live all the year long two miles up, and where Mount Illimani rises to a frightening 21,000 feet.

All of which will bring me close to a merry old age of at least one hundred and fifty. Some of it will be achieved, a lot of it will remain on the dream agenda. I do know that if, and when, I leave the New York theatrical scene, I will be leaving it in the able hands, and to the tender mercies, of Rodgers & Hammerstein, Hayward & Logan, Feuer & Martin, McClintic & Cornell, Aldrich & Myers. I will greatly miss the good manners of Brooks Atkinson in the seat just across the aisle; the jaunty appearances of Herbert Bayard Swope, editor turned first-nighter; the enthusiasms of Harry Fromkes, who spent $200,000 on *The Green Pastures* revival because he thought somebody should, and the telephone voice of Edward Morange, once of the renowned scenery-making firm of Gates & Morange, which served the American theater ever so ably before that specialist of modern times, the designer, had ever come upon the scene.

I well know, and have known for some time, that there is a pull-back to my native state of Georgia, and it's heightened, of course, by my finding of Becky Franklin in Atlanta, and in achieving a marriage that is as tender as it is solid. I've been finding that trips to the South have been increasingly exciting in recent years, and I've become aware of a new sense of values. Those drowsy Georgia hamlets have somehow become more appealing than they ever were; the people seem so genuinely hospitable. I've developed a sharper appreciation for the beauty of the red-clay hills and yellow pines, a new understanding for the life in slow motion about the courthouse squares.

I've found, too, that my feeling for the long-lost sawmill town of Olympia and its associations has been greatly intensified as the days of Olympia's glories have receded further into the past. Perhaps I'm now thinking and writing in terms of a second-act dream sequence but I've often wondered if I couldn't do something about restoring and re-creating Olympia and putting some of the original inhabitants back in Lowndes County. Decades have fled by, many of the Olympians of my boyhood have passed on, but there are scores of them still living and walking around, scattered here and there, and the beautiful Withlacoochee remains as close to their hearts as it does to mine.

Only recently, just a few weeks before these lines were written, I went back to the pines and the palmettos, to the scene of the obliterated Olympia, on a mission of recapture and rediscovery—went to stay for an hour and remained for a day. I drove along the rutted road from Clyattville, crossed the railroad tracks, and stood in the weeds before the mean shack that has been erected upon the site of Sister Mattie's fine house, destroyed by fire many years ago. The hideous little structure that now occupies the Bowen knoll and the shattered remnants of the old Negro church down near the Blue Sink serve now as markers of a cherished ground, of reminders of a town that used to be.

I recrossed the railroad tracks and then followed a familiar road that took me through the quiet pines and came out at the river's edge, just alongside the gnarled and rickety but still serviceable railroad trestle. I sat down upon a stump and didn't move for an hour.

There was great serenity. A faint murmur came from the Withlacoochee as it whirled and eddied; it was shallow, as always, around the sandy banks, and deep and swift and enigmatic in midchannel. The willows had retained their symmetry and melancholy beauty; the sun flashed its shafts obliquely through the green leaves, twigs, and burnished branches. The air was soft. I was quite alone in a great expanse of sky, sand, stumps, pines, scrub oaks, honeysuckle. It all seemed only the other day when I'd come down to the very slope, barefooted and with pole and line and earthworms—only a few yesterdays since Joe Roberts had gone to his death in midstream, just around the river's bend, and within sight of us all.

I was taken, in these hours of solitude, to the Olympia that was—the hum of the busy sawmill as the great logs were hauled up from the millpond; Sister Mattie in her bright organdy pumping away at the church organ and the congregation shrilling out Uncle Solon's favorite hymns, "Abide With Me" and "Holy, Holy, Holy"; the lovely Beulah, with her curls and plump legs, causing a hush in the commissary as she appeared in the door; the wails of the Negroes as the baptizing went along at the Blue Sink. . . . It was gone. Gone.

My reverie was broken by a blast from a locomotive far down the tracks, on its way from Madison and Valdosta-bound. I looked at the aging and shaky trestle and wondered if it could take the load.

Smoke spiraled above the pine tops a few hundred yards away, blackening the sky. There was another blast, more piercing this time. Minutes passed. Finally, the black round face of an undersized locomotive, aggressive in its very antiquity, showed itself as the tracks leveled off for the trestle approach. The angry old engine, dragging a few freight cars and a warped and rotting passenger car, slowed down to a perceptible crawl as it reached the cracked structure spanning the river. The locomotive inched forward until its full weight was upon it. The trestle creaked and swayed—but it held. The engineer

239

stared at me from the high tracks, probably startled at the sight of a human being beside the lonely river. When he reached the midway point and seemed certain that he could make it, he waved to me and I waved back. Then he gradually moved past with his sorry little train, the emergency over, and he was off on the run over the safe and flat terrain to Valdosta.

I climbed the embankment and walked along over the hot ties for half a mile to the former townsite and went again to the weeds and the crude shack on the Bowen knoll. It was there that Sister Mattie used to lift her soprano to the soulful strains of "Sweet Genevieve" and to the quicker tempo, and all the recklessness, of "Waltz Me Around Again, Willie." I went on down to the millpond, now shallow and shrunken and stagnant, its slime and blackness given an ironic touch by a cluster of water lilies in full bloom in the very center. Loose piles of bricks, grotesque heaps of rusted mill machinery, were scattered here and there. A few logs, brought in for sawing many years before, lay desolate upon the damp ground at the edge of the pond.

It was late afternoon when I walked back to the river and got into my car. There were tears in my eyes, as I might have known there would be, as I drove along the deeply rutted road through the pines and the honeysuckle to Clyattville. Those tears were still there as I reached the paved highway and moved toward the jolting modernity of the city of Valdosta— bustling, unheeding, and seemingly unaware that a blissful sawmill town, Olympia-on-the-Withlacoochee, had been born, had flourished, and had died just 15 miles away.